ALSO BY DAVID HELLER

The Children's God

The Pleasures of Psychology

Dear God: Children's Letters to God

Talking to Your Child About God

Dear God, What Religion Were the Dinosaurs?

The Soul of a Man

*Mr. President, Why Don't You Paint
Your White House Another Color!*

"Growing Up
Isn't Hard to Do if
You Start Out
as a Kid"

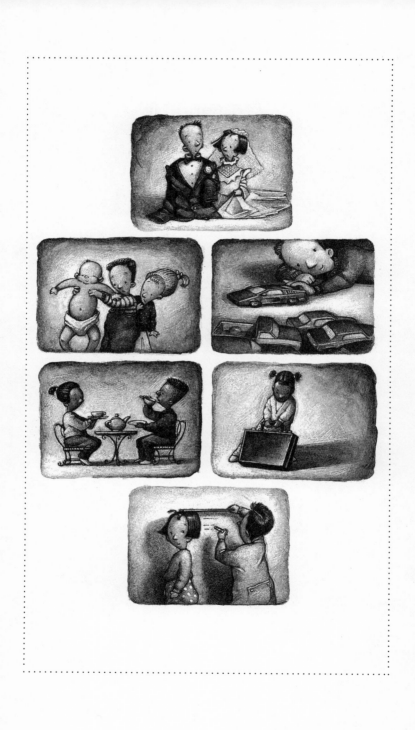

"Growing Up Isn't Hard to Do if You Start Out as a Kid"

Children's Candid Views of Everyday Life

David Heller

VILLARD BOOKS
NEW YORK
1991

Library of Congress Cataloging-in-Publication Data
Heller, David.
"Growing up isn't hard to do if
you start out as a kid"/by David Heller.
p.   cm.
ISBN 0-394-58713-8
1. Children—United States—Attitudes.
2. Parent and child—United States.
I. Title.
HQ772.5.H57 1991
305.23—dc20   90-43575

Manufactured in the United States of America
9 8 7 6 5 4 3 2
First Edition

Acknowledgments

I will always be indebted to the wonderful children whose comments about life and the grown-up world grace these pages. Their considerable spirit, lightheartedness, and candor were a joy to behold, and I am thankful for the opportunity to pass along their ideas. I have tried to capture their innocence and honesty as best as I could, and I hope that this book conveys how truly rich and imaginative they are. I am also grateful to their parents, teachers, and principals, who helped in making arrangements for the interviews.

I want to express my deep appreciation to Diane Reverand of Villard Books, who was instrumental in developing the project and who helped carry it through to fruition. Diane has great creative vision and refreshing perceptiveness, and both were demonstrated again and again as we discussed the most compelling subjects to include. I look forward to a long and enjoyable editorial relationship with her.

I am also pleased to acknowledge Elizabeth Heller, who is very wise about how children feel about things and who also happens to be my wife. Liz was involved with every aspect of the project and served as my unofficial consultant. In addition to her considerable involvement with the material, she also created the right mood for me as I was working. Thanks to her, my surroundings include a giant pencil and oversized yellow pad, several cheerleader dolls, two miniature dollhouses and their miniature occupants, a pair of dinosaur mugs, a toddler's hockey stick and puck, two shepherd bears, and an assortment of other children's toys.

Such a delightful ambience reminds me, and perhaps may remind other grown-ups too, that surrounding yourself with children and their things is not a bad way at all to live your life. They will make you happy, they will make you laugh, and just when you think you've seen or heard everything, they will warm your heart with tenderness and love.

Contents

Prologue:
Talking to Kids

Children are very good company. You can talk to them about anything. Ask them how the world is doing these days, and they will give you a blunt and honest answer without blinking an eye. Ask children about their own lives, and they will captivate you with story after story about the rigors of family life. Whatever your particular interests, children are wonderful conversationalists—not only because they say the unexpected, but because they also say the most entertaining and scandalous things.

During the past five years, I have been privy to children's uncanny ability to gab and philosophize. I began by interviewing youngsters about their views of God and soon learned through the children that religion need not always be a solemn matter. The youngsters' interview responses and their letters to God were often funny and charming. My work with the kids became the springboard for several books, including the *Dear God* series, which presents the lighter side of children's religious notions. I then moved on to the political realm and sought the opinions of youngsters concerning the presidency. I found that children's fantasies of White House life are rich and outrageous; no public official or spouse is above their hilarious scrutiny. Much of the children's ideas are presented in another book, *Mr. President, Why Don't You Paint Your White House Another Color!*

After completing these projects, I began to wonder about people and things that are more a part of the youngster's immediate surroundings. What would these pint-sized observers have to say about authority figures who, unlike the President or God, are not in faraway places like Washington or heaven? What humorous and insightful comments would they make about their own parents, other adults, and the adult world that these grown-ups represent?

With these questions in mind, I decided to study children's views of the grown-up world—the subject of this book. I became interested in not only how the children saw their parents and other adults, but also what the youngsters thought they themselves would be like when they grew up. By focusing on adult institutions and habits, I strongly believed that children would naturally share their candid opinions about the very process of growing up itself.

With the assistance of several public school systems, I gained the voluntary participation of hundreds of youngsters between the ages of four and ten. In sitting down with each child for an hour or two, I soon discovered that most children want to share their ideas about everyday life, as long as a listener respects their views and does not grow anxious when they become playful and loosen up. In each child there is a budding philosopher, as well as a comedian, ready to express himself or herself if we ask the questions that unlock their hidden treasure of original ideas.

But what subjects would offer the most interesting conversations with youngsters? I decided to concentrate on seven subjects that I thought children would enjoy talking about and the rest of us would find intriguing. Each topic is an important part of our day-to-day life.

Marriage is the first topic I selected, and this always-controversial subject leads off the book. When talking about conjugal relations, kids have the unique opportunity to play psychologist and gossip columnist at the same time. The mere mention of marriage prompts youngsters to explore the relationship between the sexes and those wonderful, awful tensions we all experience during a first kiss. It allows children to wrestle and play with the nature of intimacy among adults, and their thoughtful ideas about closeness are both poignant and amusing.

When I considered how children might perceive adults, parenthood was as important as marriage. The topic of parenthood gives children a chance to report on parent-child interaction and then a chance to switch gears and play the role of parent themselves. It allows them to freely discuss their own parents and to philosophize about how a parent should behave. Thinking about parenthood is also a way for youngsters to wrestle with adult responsibilities for the first time.

From the point of view of children, the domestic world is also characterized by the things their parents provide for the family. Perhaps no other area of adult behavior elicits as much sentiment as the provision of food. Youngsters can talk forever about which foods are a kid's delight and which ones are best rolled up in strange shapes for other, more creative uses. The children love to talk about adult foods and show off their own good taste.

In addition to food, I also asked the youngsters about adult possessions and goods. Their parents' material habits and preferences are of great interest to them. The fancy and not-so-fancy things that their parents own capture their young imaginations, as they comment upon cars, VCR's, and even smaller things like diamond rings. The children are also eager to reveal their own favorite things and the adult things they plan to own in the near future. In addition, these comments about domestic life offer a unique and engaging idea of what the modern household looks like to a child.

Eventually children begin to wonder where their parents go when their parents leave the house. What is this thing called "work"? The children approach this foreign notion with much curiosity and a bit of caution. As times goes on, each youngster naturally imagines himself or herself in a working role and even in a specific profession. The topic of work draws upon a child's fledgling ambitions and hopes for the future, and humorously tests his or her understanding of various grown-up jobs. Work also serves as another example of how children poke fun at adults, and it demonstrates how our little ones enliven mundane activities with fantasy and good humor.

Lastly, I elected to ask youngsters some general questions about the process of growing up and about differences between adults and children. The children's thought-provoking responses, which serve as the concluding chapter of the book, offer some additional insights into the child's view of adulthood. While so many of their comments are witty and humorously urbane, some of their ideas are particularly special—they make a person pause in reflection as they get to the heart of what childhood means to all of us. They make you ponder the role of children in our increasingly complicated and rugged grown-up world.

As you consider these subjects and share a hearty laugh with the parade of youngsters who make up this book, be prepared to read about some well-known parent-child dilemmas. Don't be surprised to find a few disgruntled voices among the sweet and contented ones, for the children are just like adults in the considerable variety of temperaments they unveil. That makes this collection of children's ideas all the more interesting to me, for it attempts to allow for all of the creative possibilities that childhood offers.

As you read along, you might also wish to bear in mind

the wise words of the poet Ogden Nash, who said about children and growing up in his usual inimitable way: "Oh what a tangled web do parents weave, when they think that their children are naive!"

—David Heller, Ph.D.

I

Marriage and the Other Mushy Things That Grown-ups Do

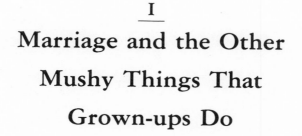

"Marriage is the same all over the world, but in some places the lady wears a big white gown to the wedding, and in other places she wears no clothes at all."
Howard, age 8

M arriage is one of our most venerable institutions. We revel in its ceremonial aspects, yet poke fun at the ups and downs of domestic bliss. The mere mention of the word marriage elicits our deepest sentiments about love and the opposite sex.

The Jewish philosopher and playwright Sholom Alei-chem thought that "marriage was a taste of paradise," but clearly not everyone has the same vision of paradise. Robert Louis Stevenson found marriage to be "one long conversation, chequered by disputes," while H. L. Mencken simply referred to it as "quiet slavery." Contemporary views emphasize the pragmatic or nitty-gritty aspects of married life. In that spirit, marriage has been pronounced "the most expensive way to get your laundry done" (Charles Jones), or as "a long bath that's not so hot once you get accustomed to it" (Anonymous).

Children have their own unique views of marriage, and their vantage point is opportune. Seated on kitchen stools or at their parents' bedsides, children are privy to all sorts of marital happenings—the silly as well as the sublime. In the midst of conversations between Mom and Dad, children learn about the vicissitudes of married life and premarital escapades. "What were the girls like who you dated before Mommy, Daddy?" they often ask. "Did you think Daddy was cool when you first saw him, Mommy?" the kids want to know. Who is better qualified to comment on marriage and dating than such keen observers of the home scene? These little ones investigate their parents' lives as if dating and marriage were exotic foreign territories, and the children accept their role as spies with a sense of grace and civic duty.

Youngsters express their opinions of marriage much as the rest of us, with philosophy, humor, and lively anecdotes based on personal experience. They expound on the pitfalls of dating and kissing, choosing the right partner, big weddings, and expensive honeymoons. They share their wisdom about a whole range of marital issues, such as what their parents have in common and why some marriages work and some don't. Then their comments take on a truly personal flavor, as the tots describe in lurid detail the kind of person they plan to marry!

Marriage is a great unsolved mystery for children. "How does it all come to be?" they wonder. Children are fascinated by how grown-ups come together as a couple, but they are not overwhelmed by the topic. When it comes to marriage they are far from silent. These youngsters wouldn't want to miss out on a chance to discuss one of the world's oldest and most controversial institutions. Holy matrimony!

What Exactly Is a Marriage?

"Marriage is when you get to keep your girl and don't have to give her back to her parents!"

Eric, age 6

"Marriage means spending a lot of time together—even if you don't want to!"

Craig, age 9

"When somebody's been dating for a while, the boy might propose to the girl. . . . He says to her: 'I'll take you for a whole life, or at least until we have kids and get divorced, but you got to do one particular thing for me.' . . . Then she says yes, but she's wondering what the thing is and whether it's naughty or not. She can't wait to find out."

Anita, age 9

"When you get married you get arranged with a man, and you find a person with rings, and then you hire a flower child, too."

Rhonda, age 8

"I don't want to get married even though I'm already nine. You're never alone and your wife follows you around all the time."

Sammy, age 9

"Marriage is when two people who have a house and kids decide to take the same name so that other people don't get confused."

Carolyn, a pragmatist, age 8

"It's when you go to church, and a man whispers something in your ear and it makes you cry, and then he gets to kiss you for what he said."

Lynnette, age 8

"To get married you have to have a big wedding where all the people get dressed up in pink and black, and they throw wild rice and they all say: 'I do! I do!' . . . Then they have a big cake afterward which the bride is supposed to pop out of."

Trudi, age 7

"I seen that old movie where they said that love means that you never say you're sorry. I think that's stupid. . . . I'd rather say I was sorry any day than get married to some dumb girl."

Glenn, age 9

"Marriage is when a boy and a girl play kissy. . . . It's okay to play kissy if you're married. You won't get arrested. . . . But if you're not married you could get in a lot of trouble."

Jan, age 6

"You have a marriage when you and a boy go to see a priest, and the priest changes your name and makes you a lady right there on the spot—in front of everyone."

Valerie, age 9

"A marriage is whatever you want it to be. . . . Like if you want to be friends, you can be friends. But if you want to be enemies, you can yell and scream and it's all okay because you're married, and you have to make up because you live in the same house. . . . Unless you get a divorce, but that takes forever and it costs a lot."

Howard, age 8

How Does a Person Decide Who to Marry?

"You flip a nickel, and heads means you stay with him and tails means you try the next one."

Kally, age 9

"You talk about life while you eat cheeseburgers and make believe that you aren't lookin' at each others' figures!"

Sari, age 8

"To figure out who you should marry, you have to close your eyes and let a bunch of them kiss you until one of them makes you see stars. . . . He's the lucky fellow!"

Melanie, age 8

"I'm going to pick a girl who walks good on the street, you can be sure of that!"

Jeremy, age 8

"My mother says to look for a man who is kind. . . . That's what I'll do . . . I'll find somebody who's kinda tall and handsome."

Carolyn, age 8

"You got to find somebody who likes the same stuff. Like if you like sports, she should like it that you like sports, and she should keep the chips and dip coming."

Allan, age 10

"No person really decides before they grow up who they're going to marry. . . . God decides it all way before, and you got to find out later who you're stuck with."

Kirsten, age 10

Concerning the Proper Age to Get Married

"When the boy and girl make six thousand dollars each."

Eric, age 6

"Ten is the best age to get married at since you aren't a kid no more."

Lizzie, age 6

"I could have got married when I was four, but I didn't like the kid!"

Judith, proponent of early dating, age 5

"Twenty-three is the best age because you know the person *forever* by then!"

Cam, age 10

"Nineteen. By then they already come with a child, and you don't have to worry about getting one."

Sandy, age 7

"Why should I get married when I can be just like my parents. . . . They didn't get married until they were both after thirty years old."

Billy, age 7

"No age is good to get married at. . . . You got to be a fool to get married!"

Freddie, age 6

"I would say that thirty years old is a good age, because when you are thirty you have gotten all your excitements out of your system, and you don't mind doing stuff like taking out the garbage."

Carlos, age 10

"My mother says: 'Don't get married till you're at least twenty-five or else you might make a mistake. . . . You can't trade the man in like he was a car or something."

Andrea, age 10

"Eighty-four! Because at that age you don't have to work anymore, and you can spend all your time loving each other in your bedroom."

Carolyn, age 8

"Thirty-two is the best age to get married at since by that time you are too old to have kids, and you can have the lady to yourself."

Craig, age 9

"You should wait till you're sixteen because it looks strange if you don't. What are you going to tell your wife if she wants you to drive her somewhere and you don't have a license yet?"

Reggie, age 9

"Some people even get married when they're forty. . . . It's not their fault they couldn't find anybody who could love 'em and live with 'em ahead of time."

Leigh, age 8

"Once I'm done with kindergarten, I'm going to find me a wife!"

Bert, age 5

How Can a Stranger Tell if Two People Are Married?

"If they are the same height or she's taller, they are probably not married. . . . Most married couples are set up so that the man is around six feet and the girl is a bunch of inches smaller. I'm not sure why, since it makes it hard for them to look at each other."

Carl, age 10

"If you want to tell if they're married, see if the man and the woman are still talking to each other."

Leigh, age 8

"Married people usually look happy to talk to other people."

Eddie, age 6

"If they are not married, the guy is usually acting real polite and plays up to the girl. . . . If they are married, he's always acting bossy and they're probably arguing."

Andi, age 8

"You can tell if a couple is a married one by whether they're wearing wedding rings on their fingers. . . . The thing to watch out for is that they might take the rings off for some reason. Like if they're in the shower. So don't get thrown for a loop. . . . You might have to guess based on whether they seem to be yelling at the same kids."

Derrick, age 8

What Do You Think Your Mom and Dad Have in Common?

"Both don't want no more kids."

Lori, age 8

"The biggest thing is that they both like the same kind of jeans."

Lottie, age 9

"My mom likes reading those romantic novels, and my dad likes sports, so I guess they must have had a compromise and decided to have me."

Paul, age 9

"They both like to argue in the kitchen."

Anita, age 9

"They both like to eat my mother's cooking."

Rhonda, age 8

How Did Your Mom and Dad Meet?

"They met at a bank. They were both cashing their checks, and they admired each other."

Tammy, age 10

"My father was walking near my uncle's house. Then my mother and father saw each other. My mother talked first, and they been talking for eleven years now without stopping."

Reggie, age 9

"My mommy went out to a disco and she bumped into him. I don't know anything about the rest of the night because that's all she says she remembers. . . . I'll bet there was plenty more though!"

Susan, age 8

"Same as most people, my mother and father met at a bar. . . . It's still a special romantic spot for them."

Lori, age 8

"They met at college. . . . I think that maybe my father was about thirteen and my mother was twelve at the time."

JoJo, age 6

"They were at a dance party at a friend's house. Then they went for a drive, but their car broke down. . . . It was a good thing because it gave them a chance to find out about their values."

Lottie, age 9

"My father was doing some strange chores for my mother. They won't tell me what kind."

Jeremy, age 8

"They met at college when she needed a date for a formal, and so she agreed to go with him even though she thought he was sloppy."

Hugh, age 10

"My father jokes a lot that he won my mother in the lotto because she's worth a million bucks. . . . But I know he just says that because he loves her and because he would give anything to win the lotto just once."

Ellen M., age 9

"They met in this galaxy, but me and my brothers still ended up weird."

> Scott R., age 10

What Do Most People Do on a Date?

"They have their first child."

> Larry, age 7

"They talk about mononucleosis. . . . That's what my parents did on their first date because my dad just had it before they met."

> Joe, age 10

"Many daters just eat pork chops and french fries and talk about love."

> Craig, age 9

"The man and the woman make a toast to each other, and it's all a downhill slide after that!"

> Cam, age 10

"A lot of people do nuthin'. . . . They just smooch as long as their lips can take it."

> Lizzie, age 6

"Dates are for having fun, and people should use them to get to know each other. . . . Even boys have something to say if you listen long enough."

Lynnette, age 8

"My sister Carol probably talks about how long it took her to get ready. It takes her three hours, and she still ends up looking damaged!"

Albert, age 9

"I don't even like girls, so I ain't the best one to give you advice about dating."

Jamie R., age 6

"On the first date, they just tell each other lies, and that usually gets them interested enough to go for a second date."

Martin, age 10

"The first thing they do is kiss, and then they talk about where to go on a honeymoon. They might go somewhere far like the Bahamas, and that's good because it gives them a chance to talk about stuff like what kind of work they do and what their families are like."

Susan, age 8

". . . . ."

"Most people talk about their families and their brothers and sisters, and then they compare who has it worse."

Howard, age 8

"Too many people on dates talk about drugs and drinking. . . . Not me . . . I'll spend the dates talking about myself."

Anita, age 9

What the Children Would Do on a First Date That Was Turning Sour

"I'd say: 'You're a boogey!' and then I'd take my bike and go as fast as I can!"

Justin, age 5

"I'd run home and play dead. . . . The next day I would call all the newspapers and make sure they wrote about me in all the dead columns."

Craig, age 9

"If I was at a movie, I'd tell her that I had to get some candy, but I'd sneak out of the movie—even if it was *Batman.* Then I'd go home, and if she called I'd tell her I have homework to do."

Cam, age 10

". . . . ."

"I'd tell him I was sick and that it was a strange disease that might be something he could catch."

Lottie, age 9

"Lose him . . . Anyway I could. . . . If I had to, I'd tell him my father came after the last kid I went out with."

Rhonda, age 8

"I would try hard to make it a good time, but if he was boring or he tried something I would scream: 'You act goofy! Get away from me!'"

Kally, age 9

"A lot of times you might need a second date to see what she's like. . . . But if I still didn't like her I would drop her cold!"

Will, age 7

"If I was on a date that turned out to be a sour time, I would either barf or die. . . . I think I'd rather die because if you barf, you're still stuck with the ugly date."

Jay, age 7

"Don't give out your phone number and there's no problem then. . . . The way I do it is I send love cards to the boys I like, and they come runnin'."

Lizzie, romantic letter
writer, age 6

A Few Famous People the Kids Would Like to Date (or Even Marry)

"Nobody! . . . I'm never gonna kiss a lady—just my mom!"
Nick, age 6

"I would like to pick Magic Johnson as a husband since he is built real good and could even build us a house. . . . Plus he's tall, and he could reach up to the roof without a ladder."
Anita, age 9

"The girls on *Star Search* would be good to look at, but I wouldn't take any of them out unless they paid for themselves."
Kelvin, age 8

"When I grow up, I'm going to marry Donald Trump because he's rich! . . . I'm ready to move up in the world."
Eloise, age 9

"I want to marry a friendly one like Gumby."
Leigh B., age 4

"I would like to date Tom Cruise because he's in a lot of movies, so I wouldn't have to work at all if I married him. . . . Also we could wear those *Top Gun* clothes all the time."

Lacy, age 8

"I'd go out with Michael J. Fox because he'd give me a lot of jewelry, and also he might like to go out with a younger girl—even if I was taller than him."

Lynnette, age 8

"I'm going to ask Paula Abdul out so I can be in one of her videos and show off what a sexy dude I am!"

Reggie, age 9

"The person I would like to date is Joey Bradley. He's a kid at our school. He's cute and he gets around—especially for a man who's only nine."

Rhonda, age 8

"I'll date any famous lady who doesn't make me take out the trash the way my mother does."

Sean, age 7

"I might want to marry Billy Joel. He looks lonely in his videos, so maybe he might need some girl company. Also Elton John is nice. Maybe he does, too."

Claudia, age 8

How Was Kissing Invented?

"It went like this: The first people had a big argument and they started wrestling, and then they kind of bumped into each other . . . in the face. . . . That's how kissing started."

Jeremy, age 8

"It was a way to get a few laughs in the ancient days."

Cam, age 10

"Kissing was invented as a way to get things going, otherwise the men would never agree to get married."

Anita, age 9

"It might have started with the movie *Gone With the Wind*."

Pam, age 7

"I'm not doing any kissing, and I'm not getting married, either. I don't like it at all. If you start kissing, you'll end up doing a lot of cleaning. . . . The men go out and do anything they feel like and leave us stuck in the house."

Lori, age 8

"I know one reason that kissing was invented. It makes you feel warm all over, and they didn't always have electric heat or fireplaces or even stoves in their houses. . . . They had to figure something out so they didn't freeze to death."

Gina, age 8

"It wasn't invented. It's always been there, and some girl and some sissy guy just discovered it."

Will, age 7

"Maybe it was the same man who invented the kite? He was a real curious type."

Valerie, age 9

"I don't know how it was invented, but it sure was a mistake. Look at all the fights it's caused in my family alone."

Tony, age 10

"A bunch of people went out into the woods and started playing dominoes and checkers, but they got tired and started looking for something else. One of them had an empty soda bottle with him, and they started spinning it. . . . The rest has been happening since, but it's still a popular game."

Paul, age 9

When Is It Okay to Kiss Someone?

"When they're rich!"

Pam, age 7

"The law says you have to be eighteen, so I wouldn't want to mess with that."

Curt, age 7

"You have to be married to kiss somebody on the lips . . . otherwise you're stuck with their cheeks."

Lucy, age 8

"It's never okay to kiss a boy. They always slobber all over you. . . . That's why I stopped doing it."

Tammy, age 10

"You should never kiss a girl unless you have enough bucks to buy her a big ring and her own VCR, 'cause she'll want to have videos of the wedding."

Allan, age 10

"Don't kiss anybody who you have no relation to, but don't kiss any of your family on the lips either. [*Who can you kiss on the lips?*] Well, like if you're on *The Price Is Right* and you win a car or a vacation, then it's okay to kiss Bob Barker on the lips."

Anita, age 9

"Never kiss in front of other people. It's a big embarrassing thing if anybody sees you. . . . If nobody sees you, I might be willing to try it with a handsome boy, but just for a few hours."

Kally, age 9

"You asked the right kid. I've kissed a lot of girls. . . . I'm an expert! It's an old hat to me! . . . What did you want to know?"

Kelvin, age 8

"I look at kissing like this: Kissing is fine if you like it, but it's a free country and nobody should be forced to do it."

Maury, age 7

"I'll probably kiss a whole bunch of girls before I'm grown-up!"

Stacy, age 5

"The time to kiss depends on who the person is. It's good if you like the person a lot, but if you don't, kissing is like having the measles or even having a worser blood disease."

Rhonda, age 8

"The rule goes like this: If you kiss someone, then you should marry them and have kids with them. . . . It's the right thing to do."

Howard, age 8

The Great Debate: Is It Better to Be Single or Married?

"You should ask the people who read *Cosmopolitan!*"

Kirsten, age 10

"Being married is better, because you can always share things with your husband. Like if you're driving and you're in a car accident, you can always say it was your husband's fault!"

Kit, age 10

"I don't know which is better, but I'll tell you one thing . . . I'm never going to have sex with my wife. I don't want to be all grossed out!"

Theodore, age 8

"It gives me a headache to think about that stuff. I'm just a kid. I don't need that kind of trouble."

Will, age 7

"Married is good because your man might help you have a few children."

Wanda, age 8

"It's better for girls to be single but not for boys. Boys need somebody to clean up after them!"

Anita, age 9

"It's better to be married so you can combine thousands of dollars together. . . . Two bank accounts are better than one, but to be honest, I might keep all the money myself."

Craig, age 9

"Single is better . . . for the simple reason that I wouldn't want to change no diapers. . . . Of course, if I did get married, I'd figure something out. I'd just phone my mother and have her come over for some coffee and diaper-changing. Then I'd say to her: 'Ma, you're the best Grandma in the whole wide world!' "

Kirsten, age 10

What Should Parents Do if They Don't Like Who Their Child Wants to Marry?

"Keep their traps shut! What do they know? They picked each other!"

Tony, age 10

"Tell their daughter how they feel, but let her decide to drop the wimp for herself!"

Claudia, age 8

"It all depends on what the parents' reasons are. For example, if they don't like the boyfriend because he's not the same color or the same religion, that's prejudice and that's wrong. . . . But if they don't approve of him because he hasn't got any money and he's lazy, then that's a very good reason. They should step right in."

Valerie, age 9

"The parents should tell the child they'll throw a lousy wedding if he goes ahead and gets married. They could threaten him by saying that they'll yell out when the minister asks if anybody is against the marriage. And they won't hire any musicians, and they'll make the people get up and get the food themselves. . . . There won't even be a big cake at the end!"

Allan, age 10

"The parents should introduce their girl to Bo Jackson and tell her: 'Bo knows marriage'!"

Lottie, age 9

What Advice Do You Have for a Young Couple About to Be Married?

"Watch *General Hospital* and see how the married couples act."

Lottie, age 9

"The first thing I'd say to them is: 'Listen up, youngins . . . I got something to say to you. Why in the heck do you wanna get married, anyway?' "

Craig, age 9

"You should really invite the whole family to the wedding. Even if you don't like them, and they drink too much and act like clowns, some of them might give you good presents."

Stephanie, age 8

"I'd tell the girl to cook stew every night because most men like that, and her man might, too."

Frank, age 9

"They should go on the Oprah show and talk about their problems. . . . It's the best way."

Anita, age 9

"First, they have to be real careful about having too many babies. I'll tell them: 'You know what to do about that, don't you?' And they'll answer: 'Yeah, we do . . . Thanks for the tip.' "

Joe, age 10

"I'll tell them to play a lot in the sandbox."

Dave, age 5

"Don't fight until you've been married for at least a week. . . . After that it's expected."

Kirsten, age 10

That Lucky, Special Person the Kids Will Marry

"Nobody! I don't let anybody near my room because that's where all my dolls are."

Sheila, age 5

"I was already married, but I divorced her. . . . She cried a lot, but I got over it quick. . . . I'm glad we didn't have to take it to court."

Curt, age 8

"It will be a fun girl from the Bahamas who moves good and calls me 'Dude'!"

Robbie, age 10

"I'm sure not marrying anybody in the third grade. They're all ugly!"

Lori, age 8

"I'll choose 'em by the hair. . . . I like brown the best."

Kally, age 9

"I don't know who I'll marry, but I'll tell you one thing— she'll have to sign a paper that says she takes out the garbage, and I get to watch whatever TV shows I want!"

Allan, who believes in prenuptial agreements, age 10

"He'll have a diamond earring in his ear, and he will have a curly high-top. After that I'll have to find out more about him because I don't believe you should go by looks."

Sandi, age 8

"My guy will have dark hair, dark eyebrows, a small nose, and even ears. Real even. Nice ones, not like Mr. Spock. I don't want no husband who looks like he's from outer space."

Rhonda, age 8

"My husband will be tall with a hairy chest. I want a real he-man. I want him to be a model. But most important of all, we'll have something the same, sort of. [*What's that?*] Well, he'll have a big mole right here on his face—just like I do!"

Corinne, age 8

"I plan on marrying a blonde actress named Kim who will be very famous, and all the guys will want her. But she'll be mine. . . . I may have to wait a little bit since she'll be busy with her films. . . . I'll give her time. I can be patient."

Larry, age 7

" I'm going to marry a boy who will love me a lot and be nice to me the way my daddy is. . . . The only difference will be that I want my lover to have long hair and a bigger car and maybe he could be a rock singer, as long as he helps clean up around our house. . . . Just like my dad helps my mom."

Marianne R., age 7

Titles of the Love Ballads the Kids Would Sing to Their Beloved

" 'I Love Hamburgers, I Like You!' "

Eddie, age 6

" 'You Ain't Nothing but a Hot Dog!' "

Rodney, age 8

" 'Shower with Me, and Don't Hog the Dial Soap!' "

Kirsten, age 10

" 'Want to Boogey with Me When I Turn Thirteen?' "

Reggie, age 9

" 'She's Like the Wind, and I'm Like God!' "
                              Paul, age 9

" 'Hey Baby, I Don't Like Girls but I'm Willing to Forget
You Are One!' "
                              Will, age 7

" 'Call Me Late at Night, but Don't Call Me Collect!' "
                              Elissa, age 9

" 'Stranger, I'm Not Smooching with You if I Don't Know
Your Name!' "
                              Roberta, age 7

" 'You Remind Me of Roseanne, so Why Don't You Get
Away From Me!' "
                              Seth, age 10

" 'Jingle Bells'—it isn't original, but it's the only one I know,
and the girl is sure to like it unless her parents just told her
the truth about Santa Claus."
                              Jeremy, age 8

What Promises Do a Man and a Woman Make When They Get Married?

"This one couple sweared that the man would never sleep with another girl or he would get zapped and die! [*Zapped?*] Yeah, he would just disappear. I saw it on a soap opera."

Theodore, age 8

"A man and a woman promise to go through sickness and illness and diseases together."

Marlon, age 10

"The people swear on a stack of Bibles that they'll stay together, but they end up getting a divorce in about three months. . . . Some people might stay together, but they might start a different kind of swearing—at each other."

Elissa, age 9

"The new married couple promises to open their mouths and let each other put their tongues in. . . . It's real gross."

Ron B., age 10

"The couple agrees to have kids. . . . Except the man agrees to it with his fingers crossed!"

Keith T., age 8

"It's something they do at every wedding. The boy and the girl have to say their vowels."

Roberta, age 7

"They take a blood oath that they'll give each other rings, and then they take a big piece of cake and stuff it in their mouth. And then, when the mouth gets dirty, their old, old mother will come over and say: 'Clean your mouth out, son!'"

Tellis, age 8

"Some people just say what the pastor tells them. But other people make up their own promises, which are usually strange. My aunt and uncle promised they'd help each other in their jobs, which was stupid because he doesn't know a thing about being a hair stylist!"

Dale, age 8

"The couple promises to share the TV and not to argue when she wants to watch a romantic movie and he wants to watch *Roller Games.*"

Howard, age 8

"I heard about what they vow on *Geraldo,* but I don't remember because there was a lot of weird spirit stuff on the show."

Seth, age 10

"I think it's strange that the people who get married promise to stay together forever. What happens when they die? What kind of marriages can ghosts have?"

Lloyd, age 8

"The bride promises that they're going to have a lot of love and be obedient to each other, and the groom mostly just keeps quiet and looks at his watch. . . . But he's almost always sweating like anything!"

Kirsten, age 10

What Is the First Thing People Say to You After the Wedding Ceremony?

" 'Don't worry, be happy! . . . And try to smile a little.' "

Marlon, age 10

" 'There's still time to get it all erased!' "

Keith T., age 8

" 'Hallelujah! I never in my wildest dreams thought anybody would marry *you!*' "

John, age 7

....

" 'June weddings are beautiful. . . . I hope you'll have a baby by July 1!' "

Freida, age 8

" 'Don't cheat on each other because that will ruin everything. Besides, you might end up with somebody even worse.' "

Wanda, age 8

" 'Gee, I always thought you'd marry some rich, handsome guy.' "

Roberta, age 7

" 'I'm sorry. . . . I hope you'll be luckier in business.' "

Allan, age 10

" 'Hi. I'm glad we're going to be new neighbors. While you're on your honeymoon, can I borrow your car?' "

Martin J., age 10

"They usually say: 'I'm happy it happened to you and not me.' "

Kenny W., age 7

" 'Congratulations! I sure hope you don't have to get married too many more times!' "

Jackie, age 7

"What everybody says is:
     'Here comes the bride, all dressed in white—
     But where is the groom?
     He's still in his dressing room—
     But what's he doing there?
     By golly, he's lost his underwear!' "

Sir Dale, the Poet, age 8

What Is Every Newlywed Couple Eager to Do on Their Wedding Night?

"The guy tries to carry the bride home and hopes that he doesn't break his back!"

Seth, age 10

"They contact all the people they know who weren't at the wedding and make sure they know where to send their cards and checks!"

Reggie, age 9

"They sit down and just sit there stunned. They can't believe what just happened!"

Kit, age 10

"They probably can't wait to go out and buy a video system together!"

Theodore, age 8

"They go right out and buy a bed, and then they make sure they break it in!"

Sean R., age 8

"They go look for a fancy motel with a giant bed and a Jacuzzi, and then they get real nervous. . . . So they chicken out and just watch a movie like *Temple of Doom.*"

Craig, age 9

"They probably try to do something together, like cook a dinner or go bowling. That way they can see if they made the right choice with each other."

Martin J., age 10

"The bride and the man go on a honeymoon, so that night they are probably flying somewhere in a big airplane and are probably afraid for their lives."

Elissa, age 9

"If it's in the summer they might go to Fenway Park and sit in the bleachers and drink a few Buds!"

Eddie, age 6

"They're glad to finally leave the parents, and they're ready to show that they're all grown up to each other."

Troy, age 8

"They eat a big dinner and make a lot of toasts, and they say: 'Let's everybody have a great time. We're glad that we got married because our parents are footin' the bill for the whole thing!'"

Clyde, age 10

"Most of the newlyweds fall right asleep, and then they wake up the next morning all shocked about who they're laying next to!"

Melody J., age 9

How to Make a Marriage Work

"Tell your wife that she looks pretty even if she looks like a truck!"

Ricky, age 7

"If you want to last with your man, you should wear a lot of sexy clothes. . . . Especially underwear that is red and maybe has a few diamonds on it."

Lori, age 8

"The way to make sure you'll stay married is have a lot of kids. Even if you have fights, you'll stick it out for the kids' sake. . . . Unless they're brats. That's different."

Lynnette, age 8

"A marriage takes teamwork. All for one and one for all. . . . So it won't do anybody any good to try to hide secrets from your wife . . . even money. But if you buy a girly magazine, maybe you shouldn't tell her, or she might be jealous of all the blonde ladies on the beach."

Craig, age 9

"Only nag your lover about how bad they look if they're in a good mood!"

Lottie, age 9

"Forgiving is important if you live together. Just say: 'I forgive you for being a louse and as cheap as anybody who ever wore pants!' "

Valerie, age 9

What Are Some Reasons that People Get Divorced?

"Divorce happens because sometimes people shoot the people they marry."

Lynnette, age 8

"There are good guys and there are bad guys. That's the reason for divorces."

Rita, age 9

"A marriage won't work at least half the time if the guy is a no-good sleazeball!"

Lori, age 8

"Some people might just get divorced, so they go on TV on that show *Divorce Court,* and they scream: She was mental and cruel to me!' "

Riley, age 9

"Divorce will happen when one person likes sex and the other one says: 'No, my head aches and my tummy hurts!' Then the first one gets mad and says: 'Don't give me any of that crap. You don't love me . . . It's all over. Let's get a divorce.' "

Marlon, age 10

"Divorce is because some people are selfish, and they hog all the money and the clothes."

Regina, age 8

"Divorce? That can be a result of the husband working a lot of jobs. . . . Like I'm going to work five jobs, and my wife might not like that. [*Five jobs?*] Yeah, baseball player, basketball player, football player, lifeguard, and then one more. . . . Maybe I'll work at McDonald's for pocket money."

Theodore, age 8

Getting Married for a Second Time

"You shouldn't feel bad if you have to get married again. Look at that lady who sells that passion lover's perfume. She's been married six or seven times, my mother says. . . . Maybe the husbands can't stand all that perfume on her."

Claudia, age 8

"The first time a man gets married he usually tries to find a real beauty, like Miss USA. . . . But if that doesn't work, he changes what he's lookin' for, and he tries to find a girl who's a good cook like his mother. . . . Then he's happy like anything, and the lady might be, too."

Howard, age 8

"Most men are brainless, so you might have to try more than one to find a live one."

Angie L., age 10

"One time is more than I can take!"

Jerry, age 5

How Is Marriage Different in Other Countries?

"To get married in other countries they do a lot of wild chanting, and they tie each other with string—so they won't run away!"

Valerie, age 9

"Some places have you donate a kid to the government, and they might not let you pick which one."

Reggie, age 9

"In South America, each man might get two or three girls."

Barney, age 7

"It's probably real wild in Mexico because it's so hot there."

Jeremy, age 8

"Most of the others get married in strange temples where they burn ashes and make sacrifices to ugly stone-head people."

Roxanne, age 8

"They might not throw rice at the wedding because they eat a lot of it. . . . Maybe they throw tomatoes instead!"

Cam, age 10

"Well, the languages are different, but the rest is probably the same. The girl looks real happy and starts crying, and everybody says to her: 'Darling, you look marvelous. I'm sure glad you married a French guy instead of some dumb American. Your guy has class.'"

Anita, age 9

"Marriage is the same all over the world, but in some places the lady wears a big white gown to the wedding, and in other places she wears no clothes at all."

Howard, age 8

How Would the World Be Different if People Didn't Get Married?

"There sure would be a lot of kids to explain, wouldn't there?"

Kelvin, age 8

"People would smoke more, because they would be more nervous."

Lynnette, age 8

"If men and women didn't get married, there would be almost no divorces at all."

Rhonda, age 8

"You wouldn't get stuck with anybody who claimed to be your brother."

Larry, age 7

"If there wasn't any weddings, that would be one less job for the priests to do."

Mary Beth, age 10

"They would have everything different when it comes to the kids. They might even have each child matched up with three adults. They could try it out to see if it worked better than the way they have it now, which has a few problems with it."

Jeremy, age 8

"No marriage? Then the women wouldn't watch their figures so much, and there would be a lot of blimps out there. . . . And I don't mean the Goodyear ones you see at football stadiums."

Allan, age 10

"It would mean my mom and dad wouldn't know each other, and so half of my personality would be somewhere else.

. . . .

. . . Probably in Chicago, because that's where my dad is from."

Ernie, age 8

"You can be sure of one thing—the boys would come chasing after us just the same as they do now!"

Roberta, age 7

II

Parenthood: The Best Way to Get Your Mom and Dad in Shape!

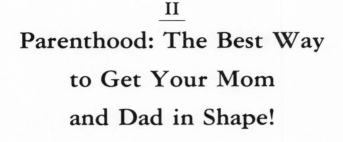

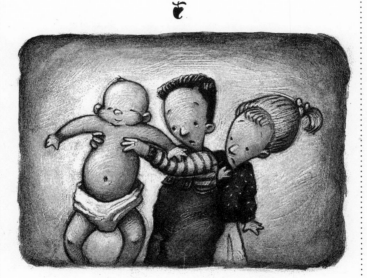

"A kid needs a man and a woman, because they do different things. . . . If there was only one or the other, the kid would only get half the picture."

Kirsten, age 10

The age-old trials of parenthood have been passed from generation to generation. Each generation complains about what a difficult chore parenting has become. Parent after parent recounts his or her own dire predicament, frequently with much self-pity and plaintive pleas for outside assistance (often from a grandparent, a day-care center, or a higher, theological figure). If there was such a thing as a universal battle cry for parents, it would probably be a resounding HELP!

What a one-sided portrait of children we get when we listen to parents alone, as they pontificate about this self-chosen profession we call "parenthood." But what about the other side of the story? After all, children have a bird's-eye view of how their parents are doing as parents.

Youngsters must have their own ideas about parenting and child care—not to mention parent care. It is high time to provide these savvy tykes equal time concerning parental behavior. If we think of the youngsters as parents-in-training, then perhaps we can all learn something from their firsthand observations about parent-child relations.

Children have much to say about why people become parents, how old a first-time parent should be, and how many children a person should have. They also elaborate on how to discipline members of their age group and how to talk to kids about sex, religion, and life in general. The youngsters are not timid around controversy either, as they delve headfirst into the hot topic of who makes better parents: fathers or mothers?

Most of what the children have to say is thoughtful and measured. Of course, a few of their comments are irascible and even irreverent. That should come as no surprise. It's been said many times and in many languages, but children do imitate their parents. Such mimicry seems to happen despite every effort to teach the little ones civility, good taste, and restraint.

What Did the World's First Parents Say When They Had the World's First Baby?

" 'Gee, Adam, how did that happen? You don't think it was all that wrestling we did?' "

Allan, age 10

" Eve might have said: 'I'm going to have twelve kids so we can have a wild birthday party every month!' "

Terry L., age 8

"The father said: 'Quick, let's teach him some sports. He's going to make us millions!' "

Reggie, age 9

"They might have tried to eat it because they didn't know what it was. . . . It's a good thing they caught on in the nick of time."

Marty Y., age 8

"When they saw that it was going to take a lot of work to watch it, they put it on a bus and sent it off to school."

Joe, age 10

"They might have said: 'I wish it was a girl. Girls are much better! Let's try again!'"

Mona, age 9

" 'Gee whiz, a baby. . . . Let's eat some potato chips and celebrate.'"

Kevin P., age 6

"The wife thanked God for the baby, and the husband went off to hunt."

Hugh, age 10

"They were in the garden, and the wife said to the father: 'My baby looks just like me.' . . . Except they didn't have mirrors then, so maybe they just thought the baby looked like a monkey."

Nancy T., age 9

....

" 'It's a miracle! Honey, get the video camera!' "

Valeria, age 9

" 'It's beautiful, but what are we going to feed it? All we got around here is those apples we're not supposed to touch.' "

Tricia, age 10

"After the girl has the baby, she says to her husband: 'Get me a tablet. Let's make a list of people to send birth messages to.' But then the husband would say: 'But there aren't any other people.' And then the wife would say: 'Oh darn, well, let's tell all the animals. They'll be happy for us!' "

Lorna, age 8

"They would sit back and relax and feel real happy, and then the man might say: 'We done it, Hazel!' "

Paul, age 9

Why Do People Have Children, Anyway?

"If you don't have children, there's not much for adults to do. . . . You can have Christmas, but there's no way Santa Claus will leave you toys if he knows you don't have any children."

Jason, age 5

"Without kids, the mothers would have to clean their kitchens on their own."

Joe, age 10

"Kids make you laugh. My little brother always cracks me up because he's only four, but he likes to look at ladies in bathing suits."

Reggie, age 9

"You have kids because you are grown-up and it's time to do it. . . . It could happen to anybody. When I grow up, I could even be some crazy kid's mother!"

Carrie B., age 8

"It's good to have children so you can be sure you'll have somebody to talk with you who don't argue with you."

Roy, age 8

"The parents have kids because otherwise they couldn't be parents!"

Will, age 7

" "I read somewhere that they used to get more land if they had a lot of kids. . . . Maybe they started doing it for the land, and then they got kinda used to it."

Brad G., age 9

"People have kids so they can write about them on their income tax and not have to pay a lot."

Paul, age 9

"Most folks want children because they hope the next generation will turn out smarter than they do and not have to work for a living!"

Tina, age 10

"If there was no kids, who else would eat the baby foods?"

Elizabeth, age 4

"You should have kids because you love them. . . . I never had one yet, but I'm going to have one soon. . . . Probably next year."

Lannie, age 6

"Children are a blessing. My parents are blessed more than most people because they have seven kids!"

Rhonda, age 8

"A lot of it is fate. If you was meant to have 'em, you have 'em. . . . And if you weren't supposed to, then you'll probably get to have something else real good—like a New Kids On the Block album."

Dom, age 8

How Does a Couple Decide When It's
Time to Have a Child?

"It happens at the same time they put up one of those signs in their car that says BABY ON BOARD. . . . Or maybe it just happens when one of them says to the other: 'Baby, I'm bored!'"

Dale, age 8

"God whispers in their ears, and their bodies do the rest."
Selina, age 10

"When the dad's wife has gotten fat, they figure there isn't much choice any more!"
Keith R., age 7

"They just have a child, or if the lady forgets to take her pill, they might even have twins."
Mona, age 9

"They eat a big meal like nachos, and then they say that they wouldn't mind having a little squirt around to help them finish off the nachos!"
Will, age 7

"They got to go out and buy a birth certificate. It costs about a hundred dollars, but you can get them pretty easy at the CVS store or some other place like that."

Kelvin, age 8

"Most people will do it if they see there's a full moon."

Jake R., age 9

"Have a child if you have an extra bedroom and you got to pay the whole rent anyway."

Carlotta, age 7

How Old Should People Be When They Become a Parent for the First Time?

"It's important for the mother to be young, like about twenty years old. But the father can be as much as seventy-five and it's okay, as long as he can still see and he has some money. [*Why the difference in ages between the mother and the father?*] Because a seventy-year-old lady wouldn't be good at changing diapers, and a young guy wouldn't change no diapers no matter what."

Antionette, age 7

"A person should be at least sixteen, so he can drive his child to the child's tennis matches, otherwise the child will have to call for a limo."

Howard, age 8

"Forty is good. . . . Any younger and you are still a young one yourself, and you won't like to look after somebody, and you might just run away to Las Vegas and play one of those lemon machines!"

Lorna, age 8

"It's all up to the parent. Some like to have their babies young. Others like to have the babies born at age thirty. . . . They're easier to handle then."

Lisa, age 8

"You might have to be more than six to have one, because I'm six and they didn't give me one yet."

Lucy T., age 6

"I want to have my first kid when I'm seventeen. [*Why is that, Joe?*] Because I want to beat out my father. He was twenty when they had me, and he thought he was real cool because of it."

Joe, age 10

"Don't have the babies until you are at least twenty-nine. . . . You have to see the good life and smell them roses first."

Kelvin, age 8

"I would say thirteen because a person, even if they're grown-up, is not supposed to rush into things."

Lizzie, age 6

On the Special Training That People Need Before They Become a Parent

"All parents should have to go to school to learn about what the right things for a parent should be. They should have classes on how to yell at kids nicely . . . and especially what to do if your little darling goes in its pants!"

Mona, age 9

"They have to find out about baby foods, and how to talk to the baby in case it don't speak English."

Rico, age 9

"First thing is you gotta know about storybooks, and the second thing is you gotta know how to read."

Elizabeth, age 4

"They should go to diaper school. It would be the smelliest school in the world, but the public schools right now aren't a lot of fun either."

Jeremy, age 8

"I wish they'd teach them how to sing. . . . My mom thinks she's an opera star, but she sounds like a sick animal."

Paul, age 9

"If you want to be a parent, you have to know about what medicines to give your kids and what to write to the teachers to excuse your kids from school. . . . You got to make it sound good even if your family is just leaving early on their vacation to Florida."

Hugh, age 10

On the Most Common Things That Parents Say to Their Children

" 'What are you, brain-dead?' "

Tricia, age 10

" 'Who do you think you are, a princess? Clean your room!' "

Anita, age 9

" 'You remind me of how I was when I was your age. . . . Except I was a complete angel.' "

Martin, age 10

" 'How is school? . . . I want the *truth!*' "

Kirsten, age 10

" 'These grades cover the whole music scale—and there's no A on the scale!' "

Reggie, age 9

" 'What do you want, little Miss Tush?' "

Leigh Ann, age 7

" 'You're really growing up fast, munchkin.' "

Laura, age 7

" 'Finish your food, dear. . . . You won't get fat from a little roast beef and gravy and potatoes and stuffing and rice. . . . I have some ice cream for you for dessert. Go ahead, it's okay.' "

Kally, age 9

" 'I'm sick of Nintendo. . . . Why don't you get interested in something that isn't a waste of time . . . like a yo-yo!' "

Allan, age 10

" 'Your father and I are in complete agreement.' They would say that even if they hadn't spoke with each other in a week!"

Riley M., age 9

" 'All right, Mr. Wise Guy, *you* put this bookcase together!' "

Steven, age 9

" 'We love all of you kids the same. . . . We just tell you to shut up more because your mouth was born moving, and everybody else's took a while to get going.' "

Cam, age 10

If a Tabloid Ran a Headline About Their Parents

"The newspaper in the grocery store might say something like: MRS. BROWN HAS GAINED FIFTEEN POUNDS!"

Will, age 7

"DERRICK'S FATHER CHEATS AT BACKGAMMON!"

Derrick, age 8

"PARENTS ARGUE OVER WHO SPENDS MORE. FIGHT DE-CLARED A DRAW!"

Cam, age 10

"DAD DISCOVERS NEW COMPUTER THAT KILLS BUGS BET-TER THAN RAID!"

Marlon, age 10

"PARENTS GO BANKRUPT! GET ALL THE DETAILS HERE!"

Elissa, age 9

"CATHOLICS AGREE TO SPEND CHRISTMAS IN BERMUDA! DON'T LET THE POPE KNOW!"

Manuel, age 10

"MOM COMES UP WITH REPLACEMENT FOR DEWEY DECI-MAL SYSTEM!"

Cedric, age 10

"PARENTS TALK ABOUT RELATIVES BEHIND THEIR BACKS!"

Alice B., age 7

"PARENTS' CAT RUNS INTO TEACHER'S HOUSE AND LEAVES A BIG UGLY MESS!"

Krystal, age 7

"NATIONAL SCANDAL! MOM AND DAD ARE GETTING ALONG TOO GOOD!"

Frieda, a steady reader of
the *National Inquirer,* age 8

"DAD LOSES HAT BUT IT WAS SITTING ON HIS BALD HEAD!"

Dale, age 8

"DARYL'S PARENTS SPEAK ABOUT HOW DARYL BECAME AN EIGHT-YEAR-OLD GENIUS!"

Daryl, age 8

"FAMILY SECRET! PARENTS PUT A THOUSAND DOLLARS IN THE BANK FOR WHEN THEY GET OLD!"

Howard, age 8

"I would have the paper say in the headline: TWO HEADS DISCOVERED IN HOUSE. . . . Then it would explain in small print that there are two heads of the house in my family— my mother and my father! . . . Everybody would buy the paper and be surprised."

Allan, age 10

Concerning Those Popular Parents
on Television

"Bert and Ernie are nice, but I don't know if they have any children."

Jason, age 5

"The Cosbys are good parents, because they fool around and laugh when their kids get drunk."

Mona, age 9

"The parents on the *Wonder Years* are real stupid, but they're supposed to be because it's the 1960s."

Bobby, age 8

"I watch a lot of Nickelodeon and the old shows they have there. My favorite is *My Three Sons.* The father there is nice for someone in the Middle Ages."

Wesley, age 8

"The people on *The Brady Bunch* should have known better and got married to the right person. That way they wouldn't be in such a big mess with all their kids."

Mike, age 8

"The father on *Doogie Howser* is a real stiff doctor, but maybe he got that way because of stress. The mother is an airhead, since she doesn't even know that Vinnie Delpino is sneaking in her house at night. . . . Where do they get the parents, anyway?"

Roberta, age 9

"Most of the parents on TV are getting paid to be parents. Mine do it because they love me!"

Sheila, age 8

Would You Like to Have Children of Your Own?

"Sure . . . Why not? . . . You got to go for the gusto . . . Plus I'll let my wife take care of them."

Kelvin, age 8

"Kids bore me. They sleep all the time like goofballs!"

Joe, age 10

"Ask me in about forty years!"

Billy, age 6

"Yeah, I'll have them . . . as long as they play the games I want to play!"

Jason, age 5

"I'm going to have about forty kids and name them after all the San Francisco 49ers!"

Reggie, age 9

"I wouldn't mind having kids if you didn't have to get married to a *girl* to have them!"

Wesley, age 8

"I'll have twins. It's easier. You can treat them exactly the same and even yell at them for the same things!"

Kirsten, age 10

"I'm gonna have one and a half kids. [*Half a kid?*] Yeah, he'll be real, real short and we'll call him 'runt'!"

Victor T., age 7

"I already plan to have little Mona, but my mother doesn't know about it."

Mona, age 9

"Sure I'll have children. I'll take them to Florida and leave them there to have fun for about a year. It's the best day-care center in the world!"

Nancy T., age 9

"No, I'm not going to have any, because it's hard and it takes a lot of time. . . . Besides, that would put too much pressure on me while I'm climbing the executive ladder."

Dana, age 8

"I don't want kids. I learned a valuable lesson from my grandmother. She's says it's easier to have chipmunks or squirrels or even ishkabobs than children. [*What's an ish-kabob?*] It's a wild animal that my grandmother made up. It has a lot of hair and screams a lot, but still not as much as children."

Sari, age 8

"Nah, I'm not interested in them. Babies are for the birds!"

George, age 8

What Will You Teach Your Children About Life?

"I'll teach the little jerks about respect for their elders, and then let them try to talk back to me or burp in my face!"

Wesley, age 8

"I'll demonstrate how to drive a car with my feet!"
Will, age 7

"I'll show the boys how to stand on their heads. [*Why not the girls?*] Silly, then you could see up their dresses."
Jeremy, age 8

"Teach 'em to be nice to people and friendly, but if you live in a bad area, don't talk to strangers and don't buy anything that doesn't have a Good Housekeeping label on it."
Kirsten, age 10

"Teach your kids to love, and they will go out right away and make love in the world."
Reggie, age 9

"A child needs to treat the parents good, but only if the parents treat him with class. . . . What goes around, comes around the other end of the house!"
Allan, age 10

"They should be nice and clean and learn to say thank you, or they'll never ever get what they want from their parents."
Lizzie, age 6

....

"I feel a parent should teach his child right from wrong, and also he should show them how to throw a baseball so it curves."

Paul, age 9

"I'll spend time with them and do aerobics with them and buy pink leotards for them so they can show off. [*The boys, too?*] I'm not prejudiced!"

Kelly G., age 7

"I'll teach them how to clean their ears with Q-tips, because nobody on earth will date them if they have yellow ears."

Simone J., age 8

"You gotta show them how to walk. The rest they can pick up on their own!"

Andre, age 7

"Teach them to love people of all colors and religions, even if some of them are boys and are inferior."

Anita, age 9

"Talk to the children about Martin Luther King and Jesus and what they said in their speeches. . . . If I do that, then

....

I won't have to think up any big ideas on my own, and I can spend my days off fishing and hunting."

Kelvin, age 8

"I'm going to teach my kids what my mom and dad taught me and just hope my boys come out different!"

Cam, age 10

What Would You Tell Your Children About the Difference Between Boys and Girls? (i.e. Sex)

"I would tell them that it's disgusting, and that would be the end of it!"

Howard, age 8

"If I had a daughter, I'd tell her to be careful and not go out at night. . . . If I had a son, you bet I would show him the ropes."

Cam, age 10

"I would tell my kids the naked truth, but it might be too intense for the little ones to hear. . . . I would start them at age six."

Riley, age 9

"Sex? I wouldn't say nuthin'. . . . They're supposed to learn that from books and magazines."

Paul, age 9

"My advice is just have your children watch Dr. Ruth. . . . That will turn them off of sex for the next ten years!"

Kirsten, age 10

"I would show my kids how to do it with a Barbie and Ken doll!"

Wendy, age 8

"I might take out a few of my *Penthouses* that I have stashed away, and the kids will be impressed with their ol' man."

Lorenzo, age 10

"I will say that they should be married first, and then they can have all the hanky-panky they want."

Valerie, age 9

"When a child is about eight, the parents should say to the child: 'Now I want you to listen good. Here's the lowdown on how babies are made.' "

Allan, age 10

"Tell your kids to stay away from each other. The girls should stay away from the boys, except if they're playing tag and they're 'it.' . . . Still, if you tag somebody or they tag you, move away from them fast, or you'll get the cooties or even worse . . . like a baby!"

Sandy, age 7

"I'd teach them everything I know, and take my word for it, that's a lot. . . . I got experience!"

Shelly, age 8

What Would You Teach Your Children About Religion?

"I might name one child Moses, so he would get interested in religion on account of he'll want to know what his name-sake was famous for."

Howard, age 8

"I'll tell them they got to find morals, or they'll die in a flood off of Cape Cod!"

Paul, age 9

"The hardest thing would be to show them they gotta believe in something that's invisible, and if they don't believe in it, they're going straight to another invisible place that's a lot hotter."

Jamie P., age 10

"Talk religion-talk with them. . . . I'd probably start with Christmas and all the presents and food, because that will get their attention the most."

Will, age 7

"I'd sit them down on the couch, and I'd sit in my big chair and say: 'They created the man and the lady before the big rest.' And the kids would say, 'Gee, that's great, Dad, but we're tired. Let's go eat some ice cream!' "

Reggie, age 9

"I wouldn't make them go to church. Some children don't like it. I know when I was a boy, I didn't take to it either."

Ramon, age 7

"I would explain to them about Jesus, and how he was a homeless person when he was born, and how we should be nice to homeless people today. . . . Of course Jesus never drank no alcohol and never bugged people for money, and there was no train stations in those days, but you know what I mean."

Benita, age 9

73

"My kids should know that there are many religions, but only one *true* religion—football! My dad says that all the time."

Allan, age 10

"I'll teach my boys and girls about the religion of sports. Basketball, hockey, tennis, softball, football—it's all holy! And soccer is the most holy of all. Because in soccer, you can't even touch the ball with your hands. Now that's holy."

Dale, age 8

"Basically, I would just give them a few pointers about God, and let them figure out the rest for themselves."

Anita, age 9

How Will You Be Different as a Parent from Your Mom and Dad?

"I might want to have my family grow up in someplace that has a different atmosphere . . . somewhere like Cuba."

Kelvin, age 8

"You can bet I'll pick better names for my children. . . . I think I'll call them Pinocchio and Geppetto!"

Mona, age 9

"I won't pick my nose in front of people. . . . I'm not saying who does."

Carla, age 6

"I hope to be exactly the same as my mom and dad. . . . Only thing that's going to be different is I'm going to spend my money on motorcycles!"

Reggie, age 9

"They have three daughters and me. But I'm only going to have boys! [*What will you do if you have a girl?*] In that case, I'll just have to cover it up."

Roger, age 7

"My parents are too easy on troublemakers like my brother. If my kid acted up, I'd turn off the TV and the stereo for a whole year and laugh in his face when he bawled like a baby!"

Carlton, age 10

"I'll be real nice to my child as long as he becomes a lawyer and makes a lot of money. . . . No reason to argue with success."

Anita, age 9

"I plan on owning my own jet and traveling all over the world, like if I want to see a basketball game in Chicago, I'll go there on Tuesday, and maybe I might want to go out to eat in New York on Thursday. [*And do you mean you would take your children so they would have many different experiences?*] What? Are you kidding? Get real! I want to have a good time. They would just be complaining and going to the bathroom all the time."

Kirk L., age 9

"I'll be a lot like my parents. I'll work hard and teach my children right from wrong, and even make them watch lawyer shows so they can learn the difference."

Howard, age 8

The Hardest Thing About Being a Parent

"It might be tough if your child is not very smart. . . . You have to be easy on the child because you don't want to hurt its feelings. You should say something like: 'So what if you aren't smart, Susie. There's a lot of other things you might be good at.'"

Shawn, age 9

"It's hard to know what you would rather have, a girl or a boy. But you still have to make up your mind when you decide to have one."

Alice A., age 4

"The hardest thing is usually getting along with your wife or husband. . . . The rest is easy!"

Kimberly F., age 9

"Drugs are the most trouble right now. Parents got to show the kids about drugs and tell them to stay away from the evil pushers who will try to make friends with the whole family. But they aren't your friends at all. . . . Whatever you do, don't ask them over for dinner. They won't just bring food."

J.T., age 6

"It's not easy to find a place to live that won't break if you have a few kids livin' there with you."

Rico, age 9

"The hardest thing by far is not to eat corn on the cob if you don't have any teeth!"

Armond, age 7

"Seeing the baby being born is the hardest. . . . I don't think I could take it. They'd have to pull me out of the room on a stretcher!"

Bobby, age 8

"Personally, I would find staying with one lady a rough one. I prefer being a playboy. . . . But I might be a good boy for the kids' sake."

Reggie, age 9

"Shopping for groceries would be a big headache, especially if you have tons of kids. I hate the stores. People are always bumping into your cart. If they were cars, there would be all kinds of accidents. They should have rules. Like the fruit lane is one-way, or maybe they could have a red light at the meat aisle."

Bucky, age 8

"The hardest thing for a mother and father is finding a good school so the kiddies can get educated. The problem is most of the public school teachers are crummy. . . . I'm sure you get the picture."

Boy's name withheld for fear of reprisal from educators, age 10

"The worst thing is when the teacher wants your child to stay back a year. The parent has to try to influence the teacher by telling her they'll help the child every night . . . and then they might also say that she's a great, great teacher and that she'd make somebody a real fine wife."

Kelvin, age 8

"I feel it would be difficult to tell your kid to lose weight if he was very fat. Especially if he's only six or seven. They don't have many diets for kids, either. So the best thing is probably to get him to run about twenty miles every day, and then he'll be too tired to eat."

Allan, age 10

Is It Easier to Bring Up Boys or Girls?

"Bring them up to what? I would leave them alone just as they are now."

Armond, age 7

"Most parents would say that girls are easier because they show you more respect, and they eat a heck of a lot less of your food."

Sheila, age 8

"It's definitely boys because they're good at sports, and girls are not so strong. . . . Unless your girl is about six feet and six inches, in which case you should keep her because you can teach her to dunk a basketball."

Dwayne, age 10

"That's a close one, but I would say it's boys because girls spend more time fixin' their heads, and you might be in a hurry to go out the door."

Kelvin, age 8

"Boys are the worst because they never listen, and they don't grow up till they're fifty years old!"

Regina, age 9

"If you're a mother, it's a lot easier to have girl kids because you can take them right into the girls' room with you. . . . But if you have a boy, that's a whole 'nother story altogether, and I don't need to go any further. . . . You should understand, Mr. Heller."

Mona, age 9

"Neither the boys or the girls are easy if they're the types who like to shoot kids at school with rubber bands and the big paper clips that sting you."

Dominique, age 7

"All kids are angels. Don't believe it if you hear something different."

Susan, age 8

How Can Parents Make Sure Their Children Work Hard in School?

"Read them educational stuff like *Tom Sawyer* and *Sports Illustrated.*"

Howard, age 8

"If you're asking for a 'can't miss' way, then promise your kids plenty of candy if they get good grades, and the kids will hit the books like anything!"

Craig, age 9

"Every parent should talk to the teachers on parents' night and find out the dirt on what is going on with their precious ones."

Valerie, age 9

"Buy the kids an encyclopedia, and make them read it if they want to get any dinner!"

Chuck L., age 8

"Call the teacher at home and have a chat with her late at night. She'll appreciate the fact that you take the time out to call, and that you don't even mind giving up your evening to talk with her."

Hilary, age 8

"Try to remember to say to your child: 'How is your work going at school? You wouldn't hide anything from me, would you? You know that if you do, your nose will grow and your hair will turn purple!' . . . This line only works for the parent if the kid's hair is not already purple!"

Allan, age 10

"Where I go to school, you don't have to work hard. . . . I go to kindergarten. Check with me next year when I move up to the first-grade teacher upstairs."

Jerry, age 5

How Would Things Be Different if Children Were Educated by Their Own Parents and Not by Schools?

"We would get really lousy grades then. . . . Take my word for it."

Rhonda, age 8

"They couldn't call it 'homework' then. . . . They might have to call it something like 'bedroom work.'"

Susan, age 8

"If we had school at home, then I could stay here where I belong, instead of having to go out into the rat race!"

Eddie, age 6

"At least we could get a decent hot meal for a change. . . . Most of the teachers probably don't even know how to cook."

Kelvin, age 8

"The children would learn a lot of bad habits, and they won't learn much arithmetic because the parents won't have a copy of the teachers' answer book. . . . You can't expect them to know the answers on their own."

Theresa B., age 8

"It would be great. I wouldn't have to go to school with girls."

Will, age 7

"You could have gym in your own backyard, but you wouldn't have enough kids for a team. Your ma might take you bowling for gym, but that would only kill about two hours, and then what would you do?"

Albert, age 9

"It wouldn't work to have the teaching done at home. . . . The parents would probably go nuts. They'd have to turn on the TV even before the kids do."

Mona, age 9

"Keep it the way it is. . . . I'm in a betting pool at school for football games, and I don't want it ruined."

Paul, age 9

How Was Being a Parent Different in Ancient Times?

"They didn't have divorces, so the parents fought it out with clubs in front of the kids."

Tricia, age 10

"In the Bible, they seemed to be real strict with their children. So I would imagine that they spanked the children plenty, or else they threatened to tell on the children to God."

Gloria B., age 9

"The kids had to help more—like cleaning up the cave or hunting dinosaurs."

Ron, age 7

"There was no television or computer games, so the parents were forced to talk to the kids more, and the kids were forced to listen."

Dana, age 8

"The problems were different. . . . There was no drugs or alcohol, so maybe the teenagers might have got into trouble by stealing camels or throwing rocks at each other."

Alexia, age 9

"The kids had to listen to what the parents said because there probably wasn't any Grandma and Grandpa around to take their side."

Holden, age 8

"The number one song on the charts was probably different then."

Anita, age 9

"The parents were more like rugged types. . . . Not like the business nerds you see now."

Kelvin, age 8

On Why Each of Us Is Given *Two* Parents

"Because they already ran out of animals at the big store in heaven!"

Paul, age 9

"They thought two was a lucky number . . . but they were wrong!"

Will, age 7

"God was trying to fill the earth with people, and He figured it would go faster this way."

Storm, age 9

"There's no secret reason for having the two parents. . . . It's just kind of a tradition that's lasted a long time."

Rhonda, age 8

"God read it in the Bible, and that's how He knew how to do it."

Lizzie, age 6

"It was a good way to fill all the homes that were built, but then they had a flood and had to start all over. . . . After the flood, they weren't ever supposed to get divorced again."

Mary Lou, age 8

"Too many parents, like three or even five, would have been a gigantic mess. With that many, they all would have been yelling at each other, or maybe having sex, and there would have been a lot of trouble and jealousy."

Allan, age 10

"A kid needs a man and a woman, because they do different things. . . . If there was only one or the other, the kid would only get half the picture."

Kirsten, age 10

Tot Tips: The Worldly Advice the Youngsters Would Offer to All Parents

"Parents should make sure they give kids lots of money, or how else can kids get you those great big presents for your birthdays?"

Lorna, age 8

"Hold your breath and count to ten the next time you feel the itch to have another little baby. . . . Remember that baby food costs money, and they don't give you much in the jars."

Kirsten, age 10

"Parents, don't drink beer or you'll have a stomach as big as a horse . . . like my dad."

Steven, age 9

"All parents should not beat their kids too much, or the parents might get all tired and worn out."

Lisa, age 8

"If your child likes a lot of action, there isn't a babysitter alive who can hold him down!"

Howard, age 8

"A good parent is one that buys a kid his own house."

Joe, age 10

"Most parents try real hard, but a lot of parents don't know how to make a kid smile or how to make a baby shut up and stop crying."

Penny, age 8

"A good parent is one who cares for the child like he is more important than they are."

Ray, age 8

"If you buy good cookies, then your children will be sweet, and you won't have any troubles."

Gina, age 4

"Bad parents come home late and wake up their kids. . . . Good parents come home late and wake up their kids to watch Arsenio Hall."

Allan, age 10

"Don't be a parent who drinks too much. . . . You can't be a mother or father or even a teacher if you do that."

Rodney, age 9

" If you yell a lot at your children, then the mayor should yell right at you!"

Rhonda, age 8

"Spend time with your children—and it doesn't hurt to spend a little dough, too!"

Reggie, age 9

"Don't make your kids eat at Burger King every night. That's no good for them. . . . Take them to Chuck E. Cheese instead!"

Kelvin, age 8

" If you want to learn how to be the best parent, I could teach you a bunch of stuff about kids—but you got to talk to my agent first to work out the details!"

Anita, age 9

"The thing that you have to have if you want to be a parent is plenty of rubber gloves—especially if your baby goes doo-dah all the time and you got a nice pink rug in your bathroom. Let me tell you, that ain't no bathroom party!"

Mona, age 9

....

"Parents, just act real slow and patient, and you can get through the parents-and-kids thing with no sweat."

Cam, age 10

"Being a parent can be a pain . . . but you have to do it if you want to be able to say: 'That kid belongs to me. I taught him everything he knows.'"

Riley, age 9

III

"Let the Grown-ups Eat Cake!" (and Other Ideas Children Have About Adult Foods and Eating Habits)

"The best food in the world is Booberries cereal because it's purple and that's my favorite color. . . . Plus there's a big monster that I like on the front."
Charlotte, age 5

"Food, glorious food!" goes the joyous exclamation from Dickens's *Oliver Twist,* and these modern-day youngsters know how to sing that refrain, too. Sure, today's children know about ice cream and candy, but don't be a bit surprised if a seven-year-old gourmet teaches you a thing or two about grown-up food. After all, children are well aware of what adults like to eat, and they are forming their own opinions about adult food.

Food is one of nature's great links between children and adults. For all of us, food elicits a great range of emotions, from profound ecstacy to that primordial and thoroughly natural reaction, *YEECH!* Eating offers us a wonderful opportunity for exploration, especially for the little ones who are eventually encouraged to put aside peanut butter and jelly and sample some morsels of adult food. In fact, one of the most endearing things about children is that they're willing to comment about a particular delicacy even if they've never tasted it.

The great variety of the world's foods unfolds as children discuss the ins and outs of fine cuisine. They reflect upon the best food in the world, as well as the worst, and they reveal to us what kind of culinary delights Mom and Dad dream up. The kids also address the comparative eating habits of men and women and offer a few tips about a subject that everyone is preoccupied with: dieting and weight loss.

These creative connoisseurs top off their wise adages with their own original recipes—mouthwatering concoctions sure to please the palate, if not the stomach! Julia Child and the Frugal Gourmet have nothing over these "child gourmets," as the kids establish that enjoying fine food is not for grown-ups only.

When Did People Start Eating Three Meals a Day?

"I think it was in 1972. . . . But I can't say for sure, since I only started eating in 1982."

Marv, age 7

"When they found out they needed protein, and they knew they couldn't get it from just eating corn flakes."

Harold, age 7

"It was in 1930. That's when they had to grow their own food for the first time."

Will, age 7

"The people in the Middle Ages got hungry. They didn't have much skin or fat on their bones, so they decided to jump from one meal every day to three. It's been a thing that everybody does ever since."

Ron B., age 10

"They were starving around when Columbus discovered America, so they had to think of something when the people on the ships were starting to complain about how they'll never see land again. . . . There was no Statue of Liberty then to let them know they were getting close. . . . The food kept them quiet."

Sheila, age 8

"It all happened in 1981 because Ronald Reagan was president, and the people started being on the street, and they didn't have enough food."

Regina, age 8

"They might have had three meals when they were working a lot. One meal before work, one at lunch, and one after work. [*When was that?*] It could have been back in the Bible days, but I'm not sure if they got off for lunch then."

Susan, age 8

"All the food companies got people to eat three meals so they would buy their products more. We learned about it in school. It was all part of the Industry Revolution."

Annie C., age 10

"People started eating three meals in the 1940s. The year before, 1939, a lot of people died. So they decided to eat better. They said to the governor: 'Governor, we should all have at least three meals! Especially the growing kids!'

"The Governor controlled the food so he called the president. And the governor told the president that the problem was bad. The president said no, but the governor yelled *'Pow!'* at the president and told him that he would tell the people.

"So the people got their food three times a day."
John B., age 8

"The three meals was in the time around Jesus. It was part of the miracles."
Martin J., age 10

"It was in the days of the caveman. One time they killed a cave bear and decided to use it for food. They had enough for three meals. So they said, 'Yum, Yummy,' and that's how the three meals got going."
Dick, age 7

"Three meals? It's going to start in the future. In my family, we never eat three meals together because we're too busy for that. . . . Personally, I eat about six a day if you count the Oreo sandwich cookies I eat at night."
Riley, age 9

"Once you stop eating the baby food and you let go of the bottle, they usually put you on the three meal plan. . . . They checked it out with science, and science told them it was okay."

Madolyn, age 7

What Kinds of Food Are the Healthiest?

"Zoo-roni! It has dinosaurs and tic-tac-toes. . . . You can't beat that for healthy food."

Carey H., age 5

"Anything that has Gummi Bears on it is good. . . . I recommend it for adults, too."

Cindy, age 6

"You should eat tons of green vegetables, and that way you won't be no weakling, and no kid will spit at you or steal your erasers or say swear words at you. . . . And no grown-up bullies will either."

Valerie, age 9

"Cheese is healthy because it's good for your teeth and gums. . . . It keeps both of them real loose so you don't have to even worry about them any more."

Cam, age 10

"Carrots can help you see. . . . Of course, if I was blind or something, I would probably skip them and eat more mashed potatoes instead."

Nancy T., age 9

"I don't see what's wrong with cupcakes. . . . People give 'em a bad name for no reason at all!"

Will, veteran cupcake eater,
age 7

"Eating healthy means no candy or cookies if you're twenty years old or older than that. . . . If you're a child, you can try them out and see if you get fat. Everybody's different, so you got to see if it's healthy for you."

Wendy B., age 8

"Popcorn is the secret to eating right because it fills you up, and it won't blow you up like a blimp—that's what happens with potato chips. They will put you in Blimp City!"

Teddy, age 7

""My advice is don't eat cholestaroil. . . . I don't eat any of it unless it's in somethin' that tastes real good."

Jeremy, age 8

"My grandfather says if you eat crabmeat all the time, you won't be a crabby person. . . . He's from Maine, so he ought to know."

Kally, age 9

"The worst thing is that stuff called wheat germ. . . . Obviously, anything with germs in it ain't good for you."

Kelvin, age 8

"Meat is not so good for you, because it's too heavy. Chicken is better, because you usually get less of it by the time your father and brother get to it anyway, and it also has less calories."

Nicole, age 9

"I eat granola cereal every morning, because it's full of vitamins and minerals, and it's a big improvement over the eggs we used to have to eat . . . Yeech! I don't care if they're scrambled or what, I hate gross eggs. The only kind I can eat are the chocolate ones at Easter!"

Mona, a hard-boiled, anti-
egg activist, age 9

What Are Your Parents' Favorite Foods?

"Most of the ones they eat are made by the place that makes Hersheys."

Harold, age 7

. . . .

"Mine don't know nuthin' about good food. . . . They don't even like Roy Rogers!"

Gerard B., age 7

"My mother and father eat all the grease they can."

Eddie, age 6

"They eat avocadoes. . . . But I think they're green and slimy, and it makes me sick to see them in the salad."

Marie, age 7

"They eat eggplant. I refuse to go near it. I tell them I'm not hungry, but I got a secret pile of peanuts in my room that gives me the energy I need."

Will, age 7

"They both like chicken, and they both like to hang out in the kitchen. . . . But my mother is a great cook, and my father is a great big eater!"

Jay R., age 10

"My mother likes this one kind of fish. She eats the eyes right out of them. I never would eat it, and I can't look when she eats. It's a kind of gray fish with big gray eyes. . . . At least they was when they was attached."

Kally, age 9

"My parents are always on diets. So their favorite food might be an apple and some water. . . . I got different taste. I like potato chips and ice cream with jimmies on it."

Ricky, age 7

"My mom eats no cholesterol, no sweet food, and mostly stuff with not many calories. . . . I wonder why she's still fat?"

Jeremy, age 8

"If you are a mother or a dad, you got to eat all your vegetables—even when they taste like rubber. How else is your kid going to learn to like them?"

Tammy T., age 9

"My mother tries to make foods that are good for all of us. Her favorite might be turkey without a lot of fat on it. She puts it in my sandwiches for school, but sometimes I trade it for peanut butter."

Ben, age 6

"Parents act like they don't like cookies, but the gingerbread cookies at Christmas make them lick their chops, just like the rest of us."

Gina, age 8

Those Exquisite Chefs in Their Families

"Let's just say we eat out a lot."

Terry, age 7

"My ma's food needs more corn chips in it for better taste."

Bill P., age 8

"My mother knows I can eat globs of food, so she always makes a lot. She calls me the 'little devourer.'"

Howard, age 8

"Both of them cook for me, and I tell them if it's any good."

Eddie, future food critic for
Gourmet magazine, age 6

"My mother makes the best food you ever tasted. That's why I never stop eating all day. . . . I could eat ten hamburgers for lunch and even more for supper. How many can you eat, Dave?"

Jim P., age 7

"My grandma makes the best pasta! . . . Maybe she would like to meet you. Are you hungry? I could bring you sometime."

Elizabeth, age 4

"I learned to cook from my mother, and she learned from my grandmother. . . . I'm going to teach my children how to cook just the same—even if I have some boys. I'll just have to start from scratch with them and show them over and over until they get it right."

Sheila, age 8

"On Thanksgiving, my father gets to play chef. He's good with a turkey, but my mom is a good cook all year. . . . But we all tell my father what a great job he did. We just say, 'Great turkey, Dad,' and he acts real humble and shy. Then we all laugh a lot, 'cause we were all collecting brownie points, and he's gonna start doing Christmas shopping soon. . . . Get the picture?"

Cam, age 10

What Does Your Family Talk About at Dinner?

"My parents like to talk about their work, but I try to change what they're talking about by bringing up all the new clothes I need right away."

Mindy, age 7

"With our family, everybody screams for more food. So I would say yes, there are a lot of conversations that we have."

Allan, age 10

....

"I try to make them talk about sex, but I usually get in big trouble for it!"

Reggie, age 9

"We talk about school, and my sister lies about how much she's studying."

Jeremy, age 8

"We could talk about how my aunts and uncles are doing, and sometimes we have them over. So we ask them how they are feeling and what they been doing lately, but we never ask them junk that might get them upset, like how much money they're making."

Danny, age 8

"We always say how good the food is, and we say thanks to our mother. We know some mothers aren't as nice, and they don't cook as good, and that can make it pretty rough for a kid."

Risa, age 8

"We always say that you shouldn't burp at the table, but sometimes I just got to."

Eddie, age 6

"We don't make small talk. We just dig right in on the steaks and have a big feast!"

Franklin, age 8

"We ask if we can have ice cream for dessert, and my father says we could because he wants some, too, and my mom always tries to convince him not to."

Ali B., age 8

International Foods I:
Do You Like Chinese Food?

"I mostly like it, but that stringy stuff looks like it could come alive any second!"

Kelvin, age 8

"Those wood sticks are fun to play with, but what happens if they ever get caught in your throat?"

Anita, age 9

"Chinese food makes you feel full all the time. I had chicken with peanuts on it once. It was good. They like to try out different things, I guess. . . . We should do experiments with our food in America, and then maybe we can start having some American restaurants, too."

Paula D., age 10

"There is a Chinese kid in the first grade. He's nice and his name is Joe. . . . But he eats the same food as the rest of us. I know because we both ate hot dogs yesterday."

Cindy, age 6

What Are Some of the Reasons That People Eat Too Much?

"They are probably trying to get fat, but you can't do it overnight."

Grant, age 8

"Because people think that Bill Cosby is right, and there's always more room for Jell-O—but there really isn't any more room in their stomachs for Jell-O."

Troy, age 7

"Every person has a thing inside you that tells you when you're hungry and when you should eat. But sometimes that thing gets broken and all clogged up, and then you think you're hungry even when you just ate a seven-course meal."

Matthew, age 6

"Because the more fat you have on you, the easier it is to float when you go swimming. . . . All the swimmers do it."

John B., age 7

"You eat too much if the food looks yummy. . . . Cakes and pies will increase your size, but broccoli will never hurt you!"

Derrick, age 8

"The big people got no way to say no. They go in the kitchen, and then it's all over."

Gretchen, age 5

"It all goes along with television. You see all the fattening commercials, and then you're hooked on the foods. . . . If you want to lose weight, you should switch and listen to the radio."

Andi, age 8

"If you're sad, the food makes you feel better—but only for a little while. Then you feel guilty for eating, and you start blaming yourself. . . . Instead of eating, you should do something else. Try Nintendo. You can spend five hours doing it, and the time will fly by."

Ron C., age 10

"Many people overeat because they feel like they have a big hole inside them that needs to be filled up. So maybe they reach for one of those huge doughnuts with the frosting top on it and have a munch. But the doughnuts have holes in them, too, and so you want to eat another and then another, and pretty soon you just ate ten thousand calories."

Mona, age 9

"You might eat a lot because you just bought a box of Ring Dings, and you don't have room for the box in the cabinet. So if you eat them, you can throw the box away."

Ben, age 6

Is Dieting a Good Idea?

"No way. You got to be crazy to be doing that. You'll never catch me doing that. I'm big and strong. Want to see my muscles?"

Jerry, future exercise-show host, age 5

"Sure. You should go on a diet if you want to show yourself off in public."

Anthony B., age 7

"No, it's not a good idea. Diets are no good for you, because they don't give you enough vitamins. If you know somebody who doesn't like how they look, you should just take away their mirrors!"

Paul, age 9

"Most of the dieters eat too much starchy food. They just got to get unstarched."

Shelly, age 8

"Diets are all what's in your head. If you think like a fat person, you'll be fat. . . . Most of the time, I try to think like a rich person. Try it. It works!"

Riley, age 9

The Kids' Guaranteed Weight Loss Plan

"I call my idea the Sheila Diet. I tell my mother to use the money that she was going to use for her food and give it to me for an allowance. . . . That way she gets real skinny, and my piggy bank gets real fat."

Sheila, age 8

"I would suggest eating a fist full of termites. That will make you lose your appetite!"

Hugh, age 10

"There sure are a lot of overweight adults walking around. . . . I would just lock all their refrigerators airtight!"

Jeremy, age 8

"Drink a lot of water, and don't eat Hostess cakes more than once a day."

Anita, age 9

"You should do what I do. I eat Doritos all the time, and I never get fat. It will probably work for you, too."

Glen, age 7

"I'll just say one word: oranges. They give you Vitamin C, and they're good for you. Eat oranges and you won't feel hungry. Eat them at every meal. [*What if you get tired of them?*] That's where tangerines come in."

Cam, age 10

"Make sure you don't eat between meals. If you feel the itch, you should have it set up so you get zapped for doing it. Like tie a mousetrap to the crackers and cheese. Every time you reach for it, you'll wish you hadn't."

Mona, age 9

"Here's my diet. Eat only these couple of foods: tuna fish, Tootsie Rolls, raisin bran cereal, and toast. They're all nutritious, and they aren't a lot of calories. Of course, you might not want to eat all of them. So you can get rid of the tuna fish if you want, and the toast is something you can skip, too."

George, age 8

"Drink a lot of water. . . . You'll be going to the bathroom all the time, and you'll be there so much, you won't be in the kitchen hardly at all."

Harold, age 7

"I would say that if you want to lose a lot of weight, skip breakfast and lunch and just eat dinner. . . . You might be bummed out all day, but you'll be real happy once seven o'clock at night rolls along."

Roland, age 10

"Eat lite popcorn, and don't eat no heavy foods like other people eat, such as chicken or tuna fish."

Andrew T., age 8

How Do the Eating Habits of Men and Women Compare?

"They both eat Gerber's, and then they try big food. . . . After that, it's the same."

Elizabeth, age 4

"Men eat more beef, so they get more build, and then if some jerk calls them a name, they know what to do!"

Nancy T., age 9

"Just go to a restaurant and see. If the man is paying, he'll make sure that nothing goes to waste. The lady will be watching her figure so she'll leave some, or else she'll ask for one of those dog's bags."

Lyman, age 9

"Girls like fancier food like orderds, but men don't digest that crappy stuff."

Rod G., age 8

"Men eat like pigs. Women do most of the cooking, but they don't always like to do all the cooking, and they don't always like what they make, either. . . . That's how they get even with the men."

Kally, age 9

"Men are always the first ones to say, 'What's for dinner, dear?' And then before you could look around, they're already sitting at the table with a knife and fork in their hands."

Valerie, age 9

"I think that men eat more in case there is heavy lifting to do or there is a war they have to fight in or in case they don't like the people who live next door."

Reggie, age 9

International Food II:
Why Is Italian Food So Popular?

"I don't know. Those raviolis give me heartburn!"

Bobby, age 8

"Because you always feel like a million bucks after you eat spaghetti. . . . It's not only a good meal, but you can play with it if you can't finish eating it."

Kally, age 9

"Italian food makes your body good, so all the girls will look at you . . . even if they're not Italian and neither are you."

Kelvin, age 8

"They put sauce on everything. I like it as long as it doesn't look like blood."

Anita, age 9

"I don't eat it much because I'm on a diet. I want to be a model when I grow, and meatballs and spaghetti aren't so good for your waistline."

Debbie, age 7

"I can make some things, like noodles. I cook it sometimes, and my daddy says it's good. . . . My mommy says it's okay, too, but I think maybe she's jealous of my cooking."

Sari, age 7

"I like how they drink wine with Italian food. I've had it a couple of times. It's not as good as soda, but it's not too bad, either. The taste is okay, but you feel kind of funny afterward. They should try to fix that, and then maybe more people would drink it."

Jeremy, age 8

"Does pizza count? Then that explains it. Everybody starts eatin' pizza first, and then pretty soon, they got to try the other stuff that the Italian's rolled up out of their sleeves."

Kenny T., age 10

"We went to the North End to one of those Italian bakeries and ate one of those canaries with the cream inside that oozes out. . . . Boy, they were good!"

Harold, age 7

Speaking of Canaries, What Do You Think of Eating Animals and Fish?

"What are we supposed to eat for proteins, seaweed?"

John B., age 7

"I guess the fish might get extinct if we keep eating them. . . . Yuk, yuk, isn't that too bad?"

Dick, age 7

"People eat frogs, too. It's wrong. It's like sacrificing. It should be a big scandal!"

Matthew J., age 6

"There's nothing wrong with it, because the fish don't even know what happened to them."

Will, age 7

"I prefer eating live candy bars, myself."

Reggie, age 9

"Eating fish is all wrong, since it is not our business to go hunting around out there in the sea. We should stay in our place on land. . . . We should eat squirrels instead of fish."

Rod G., age 8

"Geez, if we didn't eat them, that would put Burger King right out of business. . . . You have to go up and say: 'Let me have some french fries and one of them juicy salads with everything on it!' "

Allan, age 10

"It makes me sick to think about how we get our food, but I don't think I'm going to change, because I like the taste of chicken. . . . Maybe I'll think of the chicken in my prayers before we eat."

Andi, age 8

"I don't think it's right. Maybe we could just kill the pigs because they're so dirty."

Marlo, age 7

"You shouldn't kill them just for fun. But it's okay if you have to for food. I don't like those big-shot hunters who go after deers just to see if they can catch them. They're real sickos. . . . I hope the deers catch them by a surprise and bite them on their rear ends!"

Shelly, age 8

The Children's Uncensored Opinion of Vegetables

"One thing I always wondered was how come they put peas and carrots together. . . . Did you ever think that maybe they don't like being put in a pot together?"

Kelvin, age 8

"Once I go to college, I'm going to be rid of them [*vegetables*] forever!"

Valerie, age 9

. . . .

"Yeech . . . I always chew 'em and spit 'em in my napkin when my mom and dad aren't looking my way. I got so good at it, I can pretend I'm wiping my mouth, and they never know. . . . I've hardly eaten a vegetable in years."

Riley, age 9

"In the supermarket, the people in the vegetable aisles all look kind of sad and hungry-looking. . . . The people in the meat and chicken aisle look stronger, and they are more friendly, too."

Wendy, age 8

"I hate anything green. It looks like something that was alive and died a gross death."

Rod G., age 8

"I never met a first grader who liked vegetables at all."

Carla, age 6

"Did you hear that President Bush hates broccoli? I don't like it either. I'm glad he finally said something after all these years because now it might be easier for the rest of us."

Susan, age 8

". . . . ."

"Those machines that chop up the vegetables shouldn't stop with just making them into small bits. . . . They should incinerate them!"

Paul, age 9

"Spinach is the worst. They tried to tell you that Popeye likes it, but that hasn't fooled any kids for centuries."

Cam, age 10

"The reason that the word *vegetable* has the word *table* in it is because most of the stuff just ends up sitting there on the table and not in your stomach."

Kaye, age 10

"I gotta whisper so nobody hears. . . . I like vegetables. . . . But I don't want anybody to hear, or they'll think I'm weird or something."

Norm, age 7

"I like squash the best because the Indians used to eat it, and I like to throw it at my little brother."

Carlos, age 10

If You Were Stranded on a Desert Island, What Would You Do for Food?

"You got to drink a lot of those pino colodo drinks to survive."

Nancy T., age 9

"I like to have my own personal jar of grape jelly wherever I am. . . . It makes me a happier person."

Michael J., age 4

"I'd call out for Chinese food! And I'd scream: 'Make sure you bring plenty of rice!'"

Kirsten, age 10

"I don't care if I starved to death, I would never eat tuna fish."

Kally, age 9

"You got to eat what you can—even vegetables."

Taylor, age 7

"I would watch TV and eat microwave popcorn and wait for that *Love Boat* ship."

Howard, age 8

"I'd make friends with the natives and trade them my Nintendo for a few turkey-and-cheese sandwiches."

Reggie, age 9

"I would look for fruit to eat, and then I'd build a hut out of straw and try to make pizza there. . . . I'd call it my 'pizza hut.' "

Mona, age 9

"If I was out of food, I'd go fishing and thank my lucky stars that some flounder fish was about to call it a day."

Bobby, age 8

"I might say a prayer for food and then go hunting. . . . If I found some wild nuts or something, it might be hard to know if they were poison or something, so I hope I'd have my sister with me to try it out first."

Mark J., age 9

"I don't want to be on any desert island. Put me on a dessert island where all you have to live on is desserts like apple pies and sundaes with strawberries on it. Nothing else. . . . I think I could make it through *that*. Yes sir, I think I could survive!"

Theodore, age 8

"I would try to be nice to a monkey and see where he goes to find food. It's good to have a friend in a time of crisis."

Harold, age 7

Selected Recipes from the Children's Own Original Cookbook

HAPPY FRENCH FRIES

· bunch of greasy french fries
· some extra potatoes
· 2 pounds of salt
· tons of oil
· be sure to give a big smile when you're done.

Created by Kally, age 9

LIZA'S LOW-CALORIE SPECIAL

· sixty pounds of sugar
· big pile of chocolate bars
· 3 million eggs
· mash it all in a bowl
· bake it at 5000 degrees
· bake it for two days
· when it's done, it tastes like brownies

Submitted by Liza,
age 7

THE JUNK RECIPE

· take four days of leftover dinners
· pour a gallon of that Japanese teriyako sauce on
   top

- that will make the junk taste good
- throw in some rice if you need more food

Shared by Jerome,
age 9

TOMATO SALAD SURPRISE

- mix lettuce, tomatoes, cucumbers, and celery together
- use some of your favorite salad dressing
- put some of those salad bread-crumbs on top
- oh, I forgot the carrots . . . add about 5 carrots and slice them real good
- Now you're ready for the big surprise. Scoop up 3 giant scoops of chocolate-chip ice cream.
- Nobody eating it will expect that!

Concocted by Cam,
age 10

THE TOUGH GUY'S BREAKFAST

- take 7 eggs and beat 'em like there's no tomorrow
- splice some Washington apples . . . maybe 6
- splice them to a pulp
- roll up a pile of dough and throw it in the bowl like you're throwing a fastball
- chop some nuts and leave the shells in, too
- mix it all up till your hands hurt
- when it's ready, munch on it and you'll say: "Boy, this is good . . . I don't need no girl cooking for me anymore"

Tested by Paul, age 9

- get some hamburger rolls and all the same
  things your mother gets to make hamburgers
- but don't use hamburger meat—use chocolate
  instead, and heat the chocolate on the stove
- put some vanilla ice cream on top of the chocolate
- add any other toppings you like such as syrup,
  which is better than the things they put on
  regular hamburgers
- then put your food inside the rolls, and you
  have a sandwich . . . Presto!
- Don't be surprised if McDonald's tries to steal
  it from you. You can share it with them if you
  want, but make sure they promise you soda
  and fries free. It's only fair.

Described by Mindy,
age 7

International Food III:
What Do People Usually Say After They Eat Mexican Food?

" 'Thanks for the great meal, señor!' "

Shelly, age 8

" 'These burritos ain't got nothing but dough in them.
. . . Hey, buddy, you expect me to leave a tip for this kind
of meal?' "

Paul, age 9

" 'Give me another bowl of those mushy beans.' "

Jeremy, age 8

" 'Good food! I'm ready to do a Mexican hat dance. Give me my hat, Margaret!' "

George C., age 8

" 'How about a free tequila drink?' "

Allan, age 10

" 'My tongue is hot like a wild fire. If it wouldn't be too much trouble, could you get me some water before I start screaming? Thank you.' "

Kally, age 9

"The people got to let off some air, but they don't want to do it in the restaurant . . . so they might go outside and say they got to stretch their legs."

Howard, age 8

"They say: 'This south-of-the-border food is better than fire-crackers! Let's bring Grandma to this restaurant! She'll get a bang out of this!' "

Dean, age 8

On the Sudden Popularity of Oat Bran

"Is that something that people eat?"

Mindy, age 7

"Oat bran tastes like dirt!"

Will, age 7

"What is it, cereal? Forget it. I'm a Total man myself."

Carlos, age 10

"It's not as good for you as Frosted Flakes are, that I can tell you for a fact."

Dale, age 8

"It's supposed to make your heart go without a lot of bumps in it. It's not good to have a bumpy heart."

Sheila, age 8

"They even put that oat bran in granola bars. What will be next?"

Allan, age 10

"Oat bran is made to have you live longer. . . . I don't see how they can know. Do they make people eat pounds of it and see what happens to them? . . . Maybe the secret is the raisins they stick in with it."

Rico, age 9

"Oat bran is not really popular. But they started a big thing on TV about it, and now everybody in the country is fooled! . . . You should ask your doctor, because he might know something about what's healthy and what's not. Ask him over the phone and see. I wouldn't try to get a time to see him, because he'll probably make you pay then."

Jeremy, age 8

What Exactly Is an Appetizer?

"The appetizers they serve in restaurants are leftover meats. Leftover meats are better, because they taste good after they been used."

Kally, age 9

"Appetizer sounds like pizza. Is that the kind with all the works on it?"

Jerome, age 9

"I don't like that foreign food because you don't know what it is—even though you're looking right at it."

Kelvin, age 8

"Appetizers are special diet foods that are only thirteen calories each, and you can pop them right in your mouth."

Clarence, age 8

"It might be the people who work in a section of the grocery store. Like in Stop & Shop, there's a guy who walks around and puts groceries on the shelves. . . . He might be one kind of appetizer."

Valerie, age 9

"The best appetizers are girls, because you can talk to them whenever you eat!"

Reggie, age 9

"It's what you eat before you eat the big meal. . . . For me, that usually means some ice cream. It makes for a good appetizer."

Randall, age 10

"It's dog food that you get in a can but is more expensive than the regular food dogs eat."

Bobby, age 8

What Happens When You Decide to Order à la Carte?

"You say it when you're doing a magic trick with food: 'Abracadabra Alacarte!' and the food disappears!"
Paul, age 9

"They bring out the food that's on fire still when you eat it. . . . You know it's coming when you see the smoke."
Riley, age 9

"That's when they roll out a big cart, and it has all kinds of desserts, such as pumpkin pie and carrot cake on it. You tell them which one you want, and then they have to throw the rest away."
Tina K., age 8

"That's when you call on the telephone, and they deliver the food right to your door. They send a delivery guy, and he brings you the food, and he acts real nice because he thinks you're going to give him a tip. . . . But today is not his lucky day. . . . If you weren't cheap, you'd probably go out on the town in the first place."
Roger T., age 10

International Food IV:
Eating the French Way

"I bet those Frenchies all eat on the floor!"

Kelvin, age 8

"Yeah, I like that food a lot. I always eat French fries for dinner."

Eddie, age 6

"I'd go eat anywhere so I didn't have to eat with my sister."

Mike, age 5

"They make French food with special spices that makes people in a good mood. . . . Then the people want to go look for a lover and kiss her so she'll go cook some more French food for them."

Hugh, the romantic type, age 10

"I like their bread, but they need a new name. French bread is too dull. . . . Maybe they could call it Paris bread and shape it like that big tower they got there. Now that would grab people's attentions!"

Gerald, age 8

"What do you mean, 'eating the French way?' Is that eating upside down? Ask something I know about . . . like pork rinds. Those are real tasty."

Sean, age 8

"When they have a French dinner, most people don't just say they liked it. They say 'Magnifico,' and then they order some more wine with French words on it. They don't care if they haven't had it before, because you got to live it up when you go to a nice place. But don't drink too much, or you won't remember how good the food was."

Mona, age 9

"I would like to try it some time, but I'm not old enough yet. You might have to blow on it first before you eat it, and I would forget to do that. . . . I could burn my mouth so I better wait."

Cindy, age 6

The Kids' Food Every Grown-up Would Secretly Like to Eat—Every Day of the Week

"I got a joke for you. One adult wakes up and says to the other: 'Gee, I had this strange dream where I was in a big kitchen, and I was eating this giant marshmallow!'

"Then the other adult says back to him: 'You think that's strange, guess what happened to me? My pillow's

gone except for this little bit that somebody chewed on!'
"Everybody loves marshmallows!"

Allan, age 10

" Most of them like Snickers bars. [*How do you know?*] Well, my mom does. She always steals them out of my Halloween bag when she thinks I'm not looking."

Terry, age 7

" Fluff. It's good with peanut butter, and it tastes better than the stuff they eat for dinner."

Shelly, age 8

" The best food in the world is Booberries cereal because it's purple, and that's my favorite color. . . . Plus there's a big monster that I like on the front."

Charlotte, age 5

" Grape jelly sandwiches can't be beat. I could eat them three times a day, but they always make me eat regular meals instead."

Karen T., age 7

" Popcorn balls! They might want to throw them at their husbands!"

Anita, age 9

"Animal crackers . . . It's good to dip 'em in milk, but my dad is too embarrassed to do it in front of us."

Lacy, age 8

"They might like to eat Sugar Smacks, but they think it has too much sugar so they eat Shredded Wheat instead . . . Ecch . . . I think that tastes like hay."

Beth J., age 7

"In the morning, they'd probably like to eat the whole box of doughnuts, but they got to settle for taking a bite out of their kid's doughnut. . . . My mom does that, and then starts moanin' about how many calories it is."

Bobby, age 8

"Most of the grown-ups I know would love to pig out on goopy chocolate cake. Who is stopping them? They should just go ahead and eat it. . . . Let them eat the cake and the icing, too—as long as there's plenty of it left for me."

Dick, age 7

What Does That Saying "Food for the Gods" Mean?

"I think those gods like to drink wine probably."

Ron B., age 10

"Maybe when it's winter, God collects a pile of snow and makes a giant snow cone for Himself."

Dick, age 7

"Hot dogs are so good even those high and mighty types might go for them!"

Susie, age 7

"It could mean that if you are God, you can get anything you want at any time of the night, and you don't have to pay for it! Anything, even champagne!"

Allan, age 10

"Food for the gods? I never heard of that one. Maybe God needs to eat a lot more to have enough strength to do the floods and healings."

Regina, age 8

"It means that some food is like heaven's food, it's so good. . . . One example would be Reese's Peanut Butter Cups."

Sheri, age 9

International Food V: What Is Kosher Food?

"It's food from the West Coast. You can't get it here."

Nancy T., age 9

"It's about one tenth of a piece of regular food, so people who are trying to lose weight like it."

Allan, age 10

"It's when they cook pot roast, and they make it well done, and everybody says: 'That kosher roast smells good!'"

Paul, age 9

"It's the food that rich people mostly eat, but everybody else would like to."

Kally, age 9

"Kosher food is food you need to put in the freezer. You just leave it in there, and you don't have to worry about it, unless it creeps out of the package."

Wendy B., age 8

"Kosher food is like when you boil matzoh, and then you put cream cheese all over it. . . . I eat it all the time."

Carey H., age 5

If You Were Going to Invent the Food Product of the 1990s, What Would It Be Called?

"*Grown-up Mutant Ninja Turtles.* They would be made of milk chocolate, but they'd be humongous, so you could get your money's worth. . . . People would give it to their lovers and friends on Valentine's Day!''

Sean, age 8

"*Candy-TV.* You would have a big TV in your living room, and you could call the TV station and order a great big candy bar, and they would send it to you through your TV set. . . . Each station would be in charge of a different food. So like Channel 5 would be the station for lollipops, and Channel 4 would be for popcorn. . . . The best thing about it is that they wouldn't need any more commercials because you'd just have a list of foods that came with your *TV Guide.*''

Dick, age 7

"*Superpower Cereal.* It would have somebody flying around on the box, and he would use X-ray vision to sell you what you want. Plus you would have to buy the cereal because this guy flying around will have fire coming out of his eyes. . . . I'm sure it will work.''

Malcolm, age 7

"*More-Than-a-Mile-Long Pizza.* You could make the dough into a mile long road and use the cheese for dirt. The yellow lines in the road could be another kind of cheese, such as cheddar cheese. Many people would want to see it and eat a part of it, but the only problem is you would have to do all your selling outdoors, and if it rained, you would have a pretty soggy pizza.''

Martin J., age 10

"*Black-and-White Instant Breakfast.* I would put different colored pancakes on a black-and-white box. You could sell it to everyone, because it would be a hit with people of all different colors."

Serina, age 7

"*Pepto-Bismol Super-Dynamic Thing for Allergies.* It would have a person and a cat on it, and they would both be sneezing. It would help you if you have allergies like I got."

Matthew J., age 6

"*Cantaloupe Drink.* It would taste good with pizza, and you might even put some pizza on the box and in the drink, too."

Carey H., age 5

"*Edible Vegetables.* This new item would be good for you like regular vegetables, but they would taste like candy and cookies instead. The kids would eat them because they taste real fine, and the adults will want to try them because they are real trendy!"

Blaire, age 10

On the Eternal Popularity of Eating

"Eating is like riding a bike. Once you learn how, you keep doing it and doing it and doing it."

Allan, age 10

"Eating and being healthy have a lot to do with each other. You should be careful about what you eat and not stuff your face like a moron!"

Kally, age 9

"People have been eating some things for hundreds and hundreds of years. [*Like which food, for example?*] Maybe like those Campbell soups like Chicken Noodle."

Taylor, age 7

"It all started when they were creating people, and they said 'Let there be light.' . . . Before they knew it, all of a sudden there was Lite food, too."

Reggie, age 9

"My family has been eating big dinners for years, so I try to keep it going and not let anybody down. . . . I don't want them to think I'm some kind of turkey or something."

Howard, age 8

IV
The Things That Grown-ups Own (Including $$$)

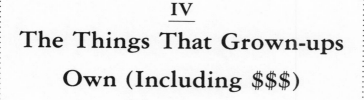

"*The best thing in life is having a swimming pool in your own yard, and no sisters or brothers you have to share it with.*"
Eddie, age 6

Our possessions say so much about us. The one thousand and one things we own reflect so much about our tastes and values. But sometimes they reveal far more than we would like others to know.

Leave it to the youngest among us to keep track of our possessions and remind us of our priorities. Homes, cars, boats, swimming pools, VCR's, and plain ol' gold jewelry— all fall within the purview of a youngster's appetite for the good life. But these things frequently hint at a child's philosophy of life as well, as some children struggle with the proper balance of material goods and more intangible qualities.

When possessions are present in a child's mind, can dollars and cents be far behind? For some youngsters, like their grown-up counterparts, money does indeed talk—and it usually says good-bye to them as quickly as it comes. For other young persons, money is a secondary concern that has its place but is not an end in itself. What a sharp contrast these two points of view create among the children!

In their observations about the material world, the children talk about the best things in life and the most expensive things, too. They comment on Mom and Dad's prized possessions, the things that are just lying around the house, and the silly things that are advertised on television. They discuss what they will buy when they grow up and what items they could do without. The children even discuss what they would do if they won the lottery, and they speculate about the exciting life of a billionaire.

It's a miniature catalog of wisdom for sure, as the youngsters tangle with small doses of greed and charity. Few family members or public figures and their things are left unscathed; mothers and fathers and certainly Donald Trump are all fodder for the children's astute observations.

Looking Forward to the Things They'll Have When They Are All Grown Up

"Maybe I'll have a couple of Hilton hotels."
Vance, age 8

"My house will have those fancy lights that hang from the ceiling. . . . I'll even have one of those lights in the room with the weights and the bows and arrows."
Nathan B., age 6

"I'll probably have two old people for parents by then."
Harold, age 7

"I might like to have my own umbrella. . . . Then I won't be so far under the one my mother carries when we walk in the rain."
Emma, age 7

"I'd like to have about two more feet on top of how big I am! . . . I could be better at sports, then."

Gerard, age 8

"I'd like to have my own space rocket—one that gets a lot of miles for the gas."

Alexander, age 7

"I'd like to own my own restaurant, and I would serve pizza in all kind of funny shapes. . . . The most popular would be a pizza in the shape of Alf's head. Another would be a pizza shaped like Charlie Brown's head, with the lines for the nose and the eyes. And then there would be a pizza shaped like a dollar bill—because I expect to make a lot of them at the restaurant."

George H., age 8

"I want to have my own place to make beer, because all the people will still be drinking a lot of it when I grow up. . . . I might try to make it less calories though."

Carlton, age 9

"I want a mink coat! Even my mother doesn't have one of those!"

Shelly, age 8

"I want to have lots of fancy dresses, and a nice figure to wear them in."

Megan, age 6

"I'm going to be an actress, and I would like to get one of those Acudamy Awards they get for being in a movie."

Paulette, age 8

"The thing I want is to have a seven-foot basket so I can dunk a basketball—maybe even backwards like Jordan does."

Colin, age 8

"I want to have many servants who will come in early in the morning and say to me: 'Care for breakfast just now? We'll bring them to you in bed. How about waffles with ice cream on them? Will chocolate nut fudge be good?' "

Bobby, age 8

"I hope to have a whole driveway full of cars, one for every year since I was born. . . . By the time I'm fifty, we might even have to park a few on the street!"

Kelvin, age 8

"I would like to own the post offices, because they got one in every city."

Riley, age 9

"I guess the only thing I want to have is my driver's license. That way I can take girls places they never even imagined was possible before they met me."

Reggie, age 9

"I would like to have a nice gold watch, because the one I got is shabby, and it doesn't even have seconds on it. . . . You lose a lot of time that way."

Sean, age 8

"I hope to get some nice rings for when I get married, and a nice husband who goes along with the rings."

Rita, age 7

"I want my own bedroom, and I want it bigger than mine is now. I'll need a lot of room for all the computer technology I'll have. I plan to run a million dollar business out of my room."

George, age 8

What *One* Thing That You Have Now Is Absolutely Essential for Your Survival as an Adult?

"I got to have my wallet near me 'cause it's full of green money!"

Eddie, age 6

. . . .

"My doll, Gwendolyn. . . . She's very good at conversations."

Daphne, age 7

"I need to get my Flintstone vitamins every day."

Cindy, age 6

"I think I could be very sad if I don't get to keep my pool table. . . . But I'm going to have to find some big boyfriend to help me move the pool table to where I am going to live. . . . I'm real good at eight ball."

Emma, age 7

"I plan on keeping my Red Sox baseball cap . . . no matter how big my head gets."

Harold, age 7

"I need Golden Grahams in the morning, or I'm no good for the rest of the day!"

Ty, age 6

"When I'm twenty, I would have to have my own airplane. I'll need it for business and just to get around the world. It will have a few ladies passing out milk and candies and whatever else you feel a desire for."

Will, age 7

"I can't be without my collection of bracelets. I need them to make me look beautiful!"

Carla, age 6

"I need my makeup kit and mirror . . . or else I might cry and complain a lot."

Marie, age 7

"Even when I grow up, I'm going to have Nintendo—I'll need it to keep up on the latest in software."

Albert, age 9

"I got to have a big yard when I have my own house. If I don't, when I throw my football for a hundred yards, like I usually do, it's going to break the neighbor's windows . . . or it might even hit their dog in the head and knock it out!"

Sean, age 8

"I could never do without flowers in the world. The smell of roses and carnations and tulips helps to cancel out the lousy smells in the world and makes you glad you have a nose in the first place."

Sheila, age 8

"I need to have two people around who make all the fine foods and tell me a good story before I go to bed."

Charles, age 7

What One Thing Do You Hope to Get Rid Of by the Time You Are Grown Up?

" I would have to give up some of my T-shirts because they are small ones, and they probably won't fit me when I'm twenty."

Harold, age 7

" I don't want to have any pimples on my face. . . . My older sister still has a lot."

Nana, age 9

" I'd give up sisters—who needs them!"

Ricky, age 7

" I could live without medicines like cough syrup, which mostly taste like you're drinking blood."

Reggie, age 9

" I'm not going to allow any vacuum cleaners in the house. . . . My mom always uses ours when I'm trying to watch TV."

Hilary, age 8

" I wouldn't care if there were no cities as long as there was mountains and lakes and green spaces. . . . Maybe they could take all the fun stuff in the city like the stores and move them out there."

Alex, age 9

"I wish they didn't have so many news shows on TV. They're boring. I would rather watch funny shows like M*A*S*H instead of hearing about wars and killing all the time."

Pam, age 7

"Can openers . . . I can't stand can openers. They look weird, and I can never get them to work. When I'm done with the can, it looks like a truck ran over it, but I still can't get the soup out."

Tammy, age 10

"I don't need no fancy jewelry to feel like a lady when I grow up. . . . Just give me a lot of nice dresses and matching blouses."

Heather, age 8

"I hope I don't have to wear ties every day. They choke you plenty, and when it's hot out, you feel like you're going to scream. My father hates them, my grandfather hates them, and I'm going to hate them, too. . . . It's a family thing."

Ken R., age 9

"If I never saw another math test, I would be a lot happier guy."

Albert, age 9

What Would You Do if You Found One Hundred Dollars Lying on the Street?

"I would buy a hundred cupcakes with it!"

Cindy, age 6

"I would give it to somebody who needed it . . . like my mother. Because she's saving for our college educations, and you can't count on a scholarship, you know."

Eleanor, age 8

"If I found that much money, I wouldn't ask anybody if it was theirs because they might lie. So I would put it in my pocket in my pants and see if somebody came to my house to claim it."

Harold, age 7

"I would hand it over to my father because he is used to holding money, and he seems to like it a lot, too."

Robin, age 7

"I'd cover the rest of the street with my buddies and see if there was any more lying around."

Greg K., age 9

"I would hurry up and open up a CD with it while the rates were good!"

Allan, age 10

"I'd keep it and buy a pair of pumped-up sneakers with it, because they cost at least that much."

Rico, age 9

"I just might buy a whole basketball arena with it!"

Reggie, age 9

"I'd fly to Australia and never come back."

Gwen, age 8

"I'd buy a lifetime supply of Bubblicious bubble gum with it."

Daphne, age 7

"I would look for the person who lost it, but if I didn't find them in seven minutes, I'd yell, 'Finders Keepers!' . . . Then everybody would know it was mine."

Brian S., age 8

"I would try to find the owner. If I couldn't find them, I might give the money to a policeman and say, 'Here, Mike. Take your family out for pizza this weekend!' "

Carl, age 9

"If I found a hundred dollars, I would give it to a homeless person, because they need it more than I do. But I would tell them to use it for food and not to talk to strangers on their way home."

Howard, age 8

"I might split the money up with my sister and brother, especially if it was right before my birthday and I knew that my mother was going to force them to buy me presents anyway."

Paul, age 9

A Few of Mom's Favorite Things

"Hairspray might be what she has the most of."

Ben, age 6

"My mom likes to have things in the shape of a heart. She's got a jewelry box like that, and she's even got a coat hanger made out of wood. . . . It shows that she's a love person, and that's why all the people in the neighborhood like her. I just love her because she's my mom, not 'cause of all the hearts."

Mindy, age 7

"My mother's favorite thing is exactly seven years old and cute as anything. . . . It's me! But don't tell my sister."

Ivan, age 7

"My mom likes tea with honey in it at night. . . . At least that's all I think she puts in it."

Rhonda, age 8

"My mom loves her kitchen the most, because she loves to cook and is real good at it. . . . Next comes my dad. She likes him, too."

Jordan, age 8

"My mother likes this standing up lamp we have in the living room. She says it's a lot like her because she's always standing up waiting on all of us!"

Susan, age 8

"My mother likes to go horseback riding. She's done it since she was a child. . . . I tried it a few times, but I didn't like it that much. The horse would never listen to me even though I was screaming in his ear."

Michelle, age 8

"Her favorite thing is to buy nice dresses. She likes to find a special one with a hole in the back or one that goes down real low and looks sexy. . . . If you see her dresses, you can tell right away that she has good taste."

Laurie, age 8

"My mom loves chocolate peanut butter cups, but she's on a diet right now . . . so her favorite thing has to be these drinks she makes three times a day and mooshes in the blender. There's some magic stuff in them that makes you look skinny."

Lane, age 7

"She has a dinner set that she likes a whole bunch, but we don't use it unless somebody important comes over . . . like my dad's mother."

Anita, age 9

"I think maybe it's my mom's shiny silver pocketbook. She doesn't like to go anywhere without it. . . . I gotta confess that I like to look at it when it's lying on the table. [*You*

....

admire it, too?] Nah, I like to see how much money she has in it."

Heather, age 8

Dad's Favorite Things

"He sure loves his golf clubs. . . . I don't know why because they don't do him much good. I caddie for him sometimes. When I do, I always wear old sneakers because I know I'm going to get a lot of sand in them."

Joe, age 10

"My father likes our pool the best, because he likes to do belly flops and show off his belly."

Eddie, age 6

"My dad's favorite thing in the house is this old blanket in the den that says on it: TO CUDDLY CHARLIE."

Howard, age 8

"My father likes football on Sundays. . . . Me? I like it any day that it's on."

Allan, age 10

"When there's a race on TV, he acts like he's a race car driver, and he makes noises like *zoom* and *varoom!*"

Jason, age 5

"Well my dad has this weird thing with his car. He's always cleaning it and pampering it like it was a baby or something. . . . I think he shouldn't be so adolescent about it."

Wendy, age 10

"My dad likes to collect magazines. He's got a lot of them piled in the bedroom closet, but I'm not supposed to see them because they're not for kids. . . . It's a waste, because we could use them to clean up the dog's mess when we run out of newspapers."

Lori, age 8

"My dad likes his glasses a lot. He thinks they make him look smart. It don't matter when I'm around though, because I always hide them so he can't do any work, and he has to play with me."

Willie, age 7

"My dad likes hammers. . . . That's all I can think of."

Ben, age 6

"My father puts this gazebo up every summer. He always makes this big deal about how great it is. When he first told me we were getting it, I was real excited, too. I thought he meant we were getting an animal like a zebra in our back-yard. Instead, we got this silly thing with an awning. . . . That's life, I guess."

Curt H., age 9

The Most Useless Thing the Family
Has at Home

"My little brother!"

> Said about one sibling or an-
> other by many children

"Our cat is ugly and just sheds all over the place. . . . Is that
what you mean by a thing that's useless?"

> Danielle C., age 9

"We have a guitar with the strings missin', but that isn't
totally useless because sometimes I hit my friend Wesley
with it."

> Kelvin, age 8

"My younger sister has a big dollhouse downstairs that just
takes up a lot of space. . . . Maybe one day I'll just give it
a shove and tell her one of those San Francisco earthquakes
happened again just like during the World Series!"

> Paul, age 9

"We don't need all the grass on our lawn, because plain dirt
would be just as good for playing baseball."

> Nathan B., age 6

Where Does Money Come From?

"I don't care where it comes from. I don't like money. I'd rather just have a lot of good toys."

Mary Jean, age 6

"My mother says it doesn't grow on trees. . . . Most of the money I have seen comes from my father."

Emma, age 7

"You just get some every week if you're good and you say your prayers."

Cindy, age 6

"Money comes from Washington. They print it up in a secret fort and then mail it express to all the fifty states. Most of them get the same amount to pass out, except maybe Alaska and some smaller states get less because they got less people. After that, there's probably a guy in each state who has to figure out what to do with the money. It all depends on where you work and what people you know real good."

Myron, age 8

"Maybe money comes from heaven, but the Devil just grabs a hold of it along the way down!"

Reggie, age 9

"Money sure doesn't come from being a teacher. That's for sure!"

Kirsten, age 10

"Money started with the Indians. I think they started printing it in the woods out of trees, and we got it from them. Since we took the land, we figured we had a right to the wampum, too. It's all a part of history."

Dennis, age 8

"Anybody can make money in their backyards if they got the right machine and a lot of green ink."

Carlos, age 10

"Most of the money comes from New York City, but I think it's all supposed to end up there when it's done, too."

Audrey, age 8

"I don't know, but I bet if you ask somebody who is rich they could tell you about ten different places they got it from."

Cynthia, age 7

"People get money from the bank. They get it just by filling out a paper. You can even get fifty thousand. You just have to ask for it. . . . What I don't understand is how the bank gets the money in the first place."

Robin, age 7

"Most of the time money comes from your mother, when she wants to sneak you a little on the side when your dad is working late."

Barry, age 9

"Most money starts out with grown-up people. It takes a long time, but sooner or later, it gets to us kids, too."

Harold, age 7

What Are Banks For, Anyway?

"I wonder if you can keep extra candy in their vaults and store it up!"

Mindy, age 7

"I'm going to put my money in a bank called Alien Savings and Trust. It will be on another planet so nobody can possibly steal it!"

Dale, age 8

"A bank is so you don't have to put the money away in your own house. Like you might put it in the bathroom, and it

could be lost because your child flushed it down the toilet.
. . . With your money in the bank, your worries are over
since there are no toilets there."

Regina, age 9

"Banks are like money stores, but they never have sales at
banks, as far as I seen."

Franklin, age 7

"I saved seventy-five cents, but I'm going to wait until I have
a dollar to open up a bank account. . . . My father says you
get more interest that way."

Howard, age 8

"How do they get all of their money in those little machines
you see on the street? . . . The people push the buttons and
they get the money. But where does it all come from?
Inside the wall?"

Greg, age 9

"Banks are there so you can get checks and you don't have
to pay with money, like if you're on a trip. The checks might
have your name right on them, or they might even have
somebody else's name on them. Those checks are good,
too."

Vance, age 8

"I know more about piggy banks. You put your pennies in there in the pig's stomach and nobody can steal it from you. But they're not all pigs. Some are other animals, and some are even human persons. I once had a bank that looked like Barbie. You couldn't get much money in her stomach because she didn't have much of one. She must have been on a diet. . . . I'm just kidding."

Monique, age 7

"Here's how it works: Your money goes in the bank and then you never see it again . . . unless you want to buy a house, in which case it goes to the house owners. It's all set up so that you can't lose it on some wild shopping spree."

Paula K., age 9

The Little, Inexpensive Things They Would Like to Own

"I want to own about six airplanes so that I don't ever got to ride the bus again . . . even to school!"

Harold, age 7

"I'd like to own a beauty place in Hollywood, so I could get filthy rich from tips by the big stars like Cher, Madonna, and those Golden Girls."

Beverly, age 9

"I want to own a college. I could be the football coach and we would play all the schools that think they're tough, such as Miami University. . . . My whole school would be made up of gigantic football players. Nobody under three hundred pounds would be accepted! . . . We'll show them all who's number one!"

Allan, age 10

"Personally, I would like to own a limousine, a mansion, and a grocery store. [*Why a grocery store?*] Because the prices of the meats and vegetables are so high, I could be able to pay for the other stuff I own."

Sari, age 8

"I'm going to own Bloomingdale's in the Chestnut Hill Mall, or maybe even the big one in New York. I'll turn them into bigger stores, and you can bet I'll double all the prices! . . . I can't wait to grow up. The suspense is killing me!"

Anita, age 9

"I would like to have a hospital. It will have twelve floors, and people will have their babies there, too. People will come in for broken arms and broken legs and broken backs, too. . . . But most of all, I want it to be a special hospital. In the hospital that I'll own, I will have a special place to treat people with broken hearts. I want to help everybody."

Rhonda, age 8

The Homes That the Children Would Like to Have Someday

" I'll have a real big house with a real big yard because there's going to be eighteen thousand kids living there!"

Jerry, age 5

" My house will have a shiny black car in it that takes you from room to room. . . . When you want to go out for a ride, the car goes through a secret cave in the cellar, and you can get right on the highway without having to stop for a stop sign."

J.T., age 6

" My house? It will be red and green, and you'll be able to see through it. The furniture will be made of cotton candy, and I'll have presents on all the tables, which will be made of peanut brittle. . . . Other than that, it will be a lot like the house I live in now."

Carla, age 6

" I'll have a nice house, and I might let my wife stay there, too, if she doesn't try to be mushy too much."

Eddie, age 6

" I'm going to build mine in the forest, so there's plenty of lumber for the thirty-five fireplaces I'm going to have . . . one for each room!"

Richard D., age 7

"My place is going to be on that *Rich and Famous* show. I'll have a special room for Spuds McKenzie so he can make it with the girl dogs there."

Ryan C., age 9

Driving Ambitions: Are You Looking Forward to Having a Car When You Grow Up?

"I already got a little car that says Rice Krispies on the side."

Nathan B., age 6

"I came here in my car, but we had to stop a lot because the car is sick. [*What's wrong with it?*] It has an infection, and I didn't get a chance to take it to the doctor."

Carey, age 5

"Cars are cool, but you can get into a crash. Don't drink and drive. Once I did, and I got in trouble. . . . It's not good to go ninety miles an hour with a Bud Lite in your hand!"

Eddie, age 6

"I'm getting my own car next year. I ain't waiting till I'm ten!"

Rocky, age 8

"Cars are too dangerous. My bike gets me around for dates."
Harold, age 7

"Trucks are better than cars. Did you know I'm going to get a big wheelie with a pathfinder for my next birthday?"
Jerry, age 5

"One thing about cars. You have to fill up your tank every year or you'll run out of gas."
Ivan, age 7

"My car is going to have a special button to push for sundaes and French fries. . . . That's what I call driving in style!"
Sheila, age 8

"They call me Fast Tony because I like fast cars and fast girls. . . . See, I even answered your questions fast."
Fast Tony S., age 8

The Pleasures of Adult Clothing and Jewelry (Or Everybody Has His Own Kind of Style and Grace)

"I'll take a snazzy shirt that shows off your muscles anyday!"
Eddie, age 6

"I'm going to wear halter tops when I'm old enough, because I know it will make the boys giggle!"

Marie, age 7

"I'm going to wear a lot of satin that shows off how pretty I am, and plenty of nice jewelry to go with it. I like to go out dancing, and I want everybody to know when I'm on the dance floor. . . . You never know, I might meet a professional man that way."

Sheila, age 8

"Most of the grown-ups wear stuff that's the same as kids, but they gave up diapers a long time ago."

Melanie R., age 6

"The women like to wear high heels to make them look as big and important as the men!"

Howard, age 8

"I would say that bow ties are the most cute on your man."

Rhonda, a fan of Pee-Wee
Herman, age 8

"I don't care what I end up doing. I'm willing to wear a suit and a tie and even suspenders and those argoyle socks. But no matter what happens, I'm always wearing

Nikes to work. I'm not giving up style just for a big-money job."

Reggie, age 9

"I plan on having an expensive watch. It's not going to be one of those cheap Mickey Mouse jobs either. . . . My watch is going to have my whole family on it, and instead of numbers, it's gonna have dollar signs . . . so if somebody says: 'What time is it?' then I'll look at my watch and say: 'It's a quarter after the big dollar sign!' "

Joe, age 10

"My mother says love is more important than gold chains and watches and things like that. I think it's a beautiful saying. . . . You know, you should follow that saying too, Mr. Heller. . . . Oh, I see that you're not wearing a watch. . . . Good idea! Keep up the good work!"

Eleanor, age 8

"I like to wear a silver chain around my neck that says BULL-DOG. . . . That's my nickname."

J.T., age 6

"They sell jewelry on television, and they always have the models come out with it and act real cool and conceited, like they're not even getting paid to be skinny and act rich. . . . If they're so rich, how come they got to be working in the first place?

Anita, age 9

"Some jewels are phony! They only look like they cost a lot.
. . . But if you talk to the person who's wearing it, you can
tell if the jewels are phony by how they act."

Reggie, age 9

What Is the Most Expensive Thing
in the World?

"A swing set has got to cost the most, because it's big and
takes up the whole yard. . . . It might be fifty thousand
dollars and ten cents!"

Jerry, age 5

"I think maybe the subway cost a pile of money."

Ben, age 6

"Some of those pictures in the Museum of Fine Arts probably
cost a thousand dollars . . . especially the ones by the guy
whose name sounds something like money. Is his name
Moonay?"

Eleanor, age 8

"The most expensive thing must be a brain . . . because a lot
of people around don't seem like they got enough money
to pay for one!"

Carlos, age 10

". . . . ."

"A computer is a lot of money, because they make some of the wires out of expensive string, which you can't buy in a drugstore or someplace like that. . . . You have to go to special stores where they have it. Look for the signs that say: EXPENSIVE COMPUTER STRINGS ON SALE."

Theodore, age 8

"The buildings in the city are millions of dollars because you got to pay for all the air around them, too."

Joey, future city planner, age 7

"The Trump Tower in New York, since it is made of all gold and other stuff that doesn't look real, but it shines a lot, like somebody's gold teeth."

Bobby, age 8

"I don't know. Maybe something real old is expensive, like something they found in old Egypt that Cleopatra buried away, because there was no bank in her day."

Anita, age 9

"A new church costs a lot. The glass that is stained with colors can cost piles of collection plates!"

Mary G., age 10

. . . .

"The most expensive thing is the Barbie Dream House. . . . It must be a lot, because every Christmas my mother says we can't afford it!"

Sheila, age 8

"I know the cheapest thing. . . . It's a bubble-gum ball. You put the coin in the machine, and it comes out. But my mother always says not to eat it, because it looks dirty and has spots on it. . . . You can't trust anything no more."

Will, age 7

"The Sears building in Chicago might be if they had to move it. What kind of moving truck could they get for that?"

Allan, age 10

"Diamonds are the most expensive, and second place might be airplanes, and third place might be mink coats, but only if they came from real foxes and not fake ones. . . . You got to pay a lot for those coats, but not as much as the animal had to, because it got killed to get you the coat."

Kris S., age 9

"The most expensive thing in the whole world might be an atomic bomb. . . . It cost many millions, and it might cost millions of people's lives, too."

Sid, age 8

"Love must be the richest thing, because you can't buy it no matter how much you save."

Reggie, age 9

On the Ups and Downs of Being a Billionaire

"Not all the rich guys are wimps. . . . Wrestlers make a lot of millions, but they aren't sissies. Look, they even shave their heads!"

Kelvin, age 8

"Donald Trump is a billionaire, but he's still got problems. Look at how his marriage problems got written about in *People* magazine, and they put his wife on the cover, smiling because she's thinking about all the money she might get— one way or another."

Valerie, age 9

"Billionaires? I wouldn't want the hassle. Give me a measly million, and I'll be satisfied!"

Myron, age 8

"I wouldn't mind owning a casino, because I like to show that I am a big sports fan, and besides, I think people should go back to old-fashioned games like card games instead of watching so much television."

Bart F., age 9

"Money isn't the only thing that counts. You have to have people who care about you and want to buy you things."

Nancy T., age 9

"The best thing about being a billionaire is that I could fly around the country, and I wouldn't even have to bug my dad once for some cash!"

Jeremy, age 8

"How much is a billion? Boy, if they got that much, they could even buy all the big Macs they sell at McDonald's!"

Tracy, age 7

"Some of the billionaires got oil. Others got land. Some others even got their own countries. . . . If I had that much money, I'd do something different. I'd own all the rivers and the oceans. That way I'd make sure everybody ate a lot of fish. They should, because it's good for them. . . . Eat fish twice a week!"

Paul, age 9

"Just because you got money doesn't mean you have everything. A person can be rich in spirit, too. Do you think anybody is a billionaire in their spirits? I wonder if we would ever know who that person is?"

Patrice, age 10

How Much Do You Think the President Makes a Year?

"If he's fair to the American people and only takes what he deserves, then I would say he should get about six hundred dollars."

Sari, age 8

"Bush gets about five million dollars. . . . That's why the people in my school voted for Dukakis."

Rhonda, age 8

"It depends on how the president does. He could get a raise if he gets along with other countries. [*And if he doesn't?*] Then he should get less money. It's the right way to do it!"

Reggie, age 9

"I don't think President Bush gets paid. He's kind of retired, so he has a lot of time on his hands."

Wayne G., age 9

"He might get free stuff like food and postage stamps, and he gets his laundry done, so that's why everybody wants to be president."

Clement, age 8

"The president gets a dollar out of every citizen's taxes, so I guess he doesn't make that much money."

                                                    Theodore, age 8

"How much does the president make? I'd say about eighty dollars, and maybe he gives twenty to Vice-President Quayle so that he can travel to other countries."

                                                    Denny B., age 7

First Thoughts on Winning the State Lottery

"I'd scream and then I'd say, 'Grab your coats, kids! We're going to paint this town green! Let's go shopping!'"

                                                    Mona, age 9

"I would be jumping on the chair and then I'd stand on my head so that I could see what the world looked like upside down."

                                                    Jeremy, age 8

"I'd think about all the trucks and dirt I could buy with the money!"

                                                    Jerry, age 5

"I'd give my parents some money for their help, and I might even give them a loan, too, if they let me stay up later. . . . You shouldn't forget them just 'cause of some old arguments."

Sid, age 8

"I might think to myself that God was good to me, and that there must be a God, and I bet He gave me this money because I'm nice to people. . . . Don't worry, God, I'll split the cash with my family!"

Gwen, age 8

"The first thing I'd say is 'Money, how I love ya!' Then I'd think of the less fortunate, and so I'd give some to my brother, because he's stupid and ugly and is never going to get anywhere in life without my help."

Paul, age 9

"I guess I might call my mother and have her come down to school in a limo, a big white one with twelve tires and eight doors. Then we'd drive over to City Hall and meet the mayor and tell him to arrange a big parade for me. . . . I'll ride in a big money float and wave to the crowds with a lot of money in my hands."

Lisa L., age 8

"Maybe I would yell and jump up and down, and then I'd say that I sure was glad I bought that lotto ticket instead of the bag of peanuts I was gonna buy!"

Bobby, age 8

"I'd treat my whole school to whatever ice cream they wanted, and only charge each of them a quarter a kid for the cones."

Riley, age 9

The Best Things in Life

"The best thing in life is having a swimming pool in your own yard and no sisters or brothers you have to share it with."

Eddie, age 6

"I have a necklace that spells ROBIN on it. That's the best thing I got so far."

Robin, age 7

"The best thing is to be happy and not ever fall down and scrape your legs."

Emma, age 7

"I wish I lived near some wild animals. That would be the best thing."

Harold, age 7

". . . . ."

"A house is the best thing in life, because no robber can fit it in his getaway car!"

Kelvin, age 8

"The best thing is having a shed of your own where you can keep your toys and hatchets and things like that!"

Jerry, age 5

"Jacuzzis are better than anything. . . . The water swishes around and even goes inside your pants, and all you have to do is sit there. . . . I never been in one, but I saw them on TV. They make them in California, I think, and then they sell them to everybody else."

Ivan, age 7

"A car is the best, since it keeps you from wasting money on taxis that cost twenty-five dollars to go three blocks."

Mona, age 9

"The best thing would be to have a silver mansion with a big silver video arcade right in the middle!"

Anita, age 9

"The best thing? It would be to own the New Orleans Saints. I hear the cheerleaders come with it free!"

Reggie, age 9

"The best thing in life would be to own a miniature doll-house shop."

Liz S., age 8

"To each his own. Some people might say money is the best, but somebody else who is smarter might say health is most important. . . . As for me, I say 'give me liberty or give me death!' "

Joshua P., age 10

"I say the best thing in the world is a strawberry sundae. But another kid might feel something else. They might say that butterscotch is the best!"

Chuckie, age 7

Is the World Too Concerned with Money and Material Things?

"Only at Christmastime. . . . Other than that, it's not too bad."

Orson, age 8

"I think that the people of the world should pass a law that says everybody should have enough money. . . . That would be good, and it would mean that all the leaders would have to fess up and share the money they got in their palaces."

Tess, age 8

"Some people are too concerned with money, but not in my family. We're liberated from money. We spend it as soon as we get it!"

Kirsten, age 10

"I can't say for the rest of the world, but my family just uses what we need. We have a nice big house, three cars, three TVs, our boat, and that's it."

Missy, age 9

"No, my father needs to think more about money so he can get me a new bike!"

Sammy O., age 6

"There is a lot of money on the earth, and I'm planning on having about half of it!"

Eddie, age 6

"Yes. We should spend more on how to cure AIDS and stop drugs, instead of buying expensive furniture and carpets. . . . Maybe if we sat on the floors more we would be closer to each other!"

Irena, age 10

"Scrooge was more concerned than most people about money, and look what happened to him. . . . I don't want no ghosts visiting me."

Dale, age 8

"You should try to love all your neighbors. . . . Even people who love money too much, such as the ones who sell cars and the ones who collect your taxes."

Regina, age 9

V

Work and Other Occupational Hazards of Being Grown Up

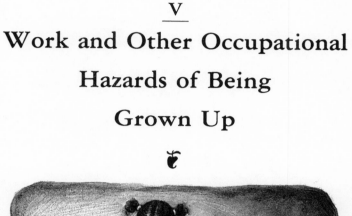

"My idea about work is that most adults are lazy and don't like to work, but they have to so they can pay for their condos and microwaves!"

Morton, age 7

Iᵗ's not that all children despise work—it's just that the ones who do are so vocal about it. There's no disputing matters of taste, and some youngsters just don't have any appetite for sweat and toil. Fun is their game, and they're prepared to play until bedtime.

These children see work as drudgery in disguise. They like being kids and are in no particular hurry to enter the adult work world. The youngsters would rather spend their valuable time on other things. But are they wasteful or indolent? On the contrary, they are ready to replace work with all kinds of surrogate activities—like kickball, bike racing, and Nintendo!

Some youngsters offer a more positive view of work. These children seem to adopt Ben Franklin's philosophy: "He that hath a trade has an estate." They are quick to tell you what careers they'll choose and equally certain about the huge homes they'll build with labor's rewards. (It seems they take Mr. Franklin's maxim quite literally.) These children are enthusiastic about their chosen professions, and they're full of fantasies about how exciting it will be to earn a paycheck.

Regardless of their individual attitudes about work, all of the children have colorful things to say about the place of work in a person's life. Among the subjects they freely discuss are the following: what they think of their parents' jobs; how most people feel about their jobs and their bosses; who is overpaid and who is underpaid; what's the easiest job in the world and what's the toughest. Throughout, the children's answers remind us that playfulness and levity are always possible for children and for adults, too, even when the subject is that nasty four-letter word called work.

What Is the First Thing You Think of When You Hear the Word *Work*?

"I see a big red factory with steam all over the place, and a bunch of people who look like slaves. . . . They're chopping on some rocks, and there's a guy whipping them. . . . He's kind of their boss, and he's weird looking. He's all red with horns sticking up out of his head."

Cam, age 10

"I just come up blank, and then nothing appeared until you said 'play.'"

Bart, age 8

"As soon as I hear the word, my back starts to hurt a lot and I get cramps in my legs."

Kirsten, age 10

"I think about how I'm going to be a baseball player and make three million dollars a year from the Oakland A's and so I won't ever have to work."

Jeremy, age 8

"If I had my choice, I'd be a beach bum and play volleyball and show off my chest to the girls on the beach. . . . I'd rather have a workout than work!"

C.J., age 8

"The first thing I think of is dollar bills . . . lots of them . . . and then I feel happy."

Anita, age 9

"I think about getting up at seven o'clock and kissing my wife good-bye, and then going off to the bank to collect some money—so I can bring home the bacon by lunchtime. . . . I got it all figured out."

Riley, age 9

"Work makes me sleepy. . . . Got any questions about fun stuff like what movies we've seen lately? I can tell you a lot about them."

Sheila, age 8

Why Do People Have to Work, Anyway?

"Because if people didn't work, many people would spend all of their time gambling all of their money away on lottery tickets."

Marie, age 7

"If nobody went to work, and everybody was home all the time, then you would have to stand in line to go the bathroom, and that could be really gross."

Mona, age 9

"Work gives you money, and that's where the real trouble starts!"

Lucy, age 7

"Work gets a person the food they need to live, such as graham crackers."

Nellie, age 6

"Work equals money equals a summer house on a lake!"

Milt, age 9

"You can learn things through work. . . . For example, you can learn that you don't like what you're doing and you would rather inherit a fortune!"

Valerie, age 9

"People work because it's supposed to be good for you. . . . But I ain't figured out *how* it's supposed to be good for you!"

Will, age 7

"You got to work so you can have a family, because they won't want you as a father if you don't have a job."

Kelvin, age 8

"Work might make you a better person, because after you work all day, you might fall right asleep, and there's no way you can get into an argument with your wife."

Bobby, age 8

"Most people work 'cause they love to do it. That's why I'm going to be a race car driver. . . . Look me up at the Indianapolis 500. I'll be smiling because I just won, and I just saw the checkered flag."

Rich G., future protégé of
Mario Andretti, age 10

"Work keeps you busy and so you don't waste any time. . . . Plus you might make friends at work—even if you're a lawyer like my uncle and you are supposed to argue it out with everybody."

Sari, age 8

"I don't know what work does for other moms, but it makes my mom a nervous wreck . . . and you can quote me on it!"
Lauren T., age 8

The Best Kind of Work in the Whole Wide World

"Being in the circus is neat. . . . It's fun, and you can learn how to do tricks, and you can get into funny positions with the animals, and most of them are good for kids to see."
Howard, age 8

"The best job in the world is being a king, but I get the feeling that those jobs are hard to get in this day and age."
Lorenzo, age 8

"Santa Claus's work is not bad, since you get to make people happy and you only have to work for one day a year. . . . The bad thing about it is that you would have to put up with all the fake Santa Clauses in all the shopping malls."
Claire, age 7

"The best thing to do is owning a car dealership on Auto Mile, since you can drive a different car every day."
Kelvin, age 8

"The sports announcers have good jobs, because they go to all the games without having to pay. . . . People listen to whatever they say, even if they don't know what they're talking about."

Joe, age 10

"The best job in the world is being a mom. . . . You don't get paid anything, but at least when you're a mom, there's no higher boss you have to answer to!"

Mona, age 9

"Selling things is the best. I want to learn a lot about it. . . . When I going grow up, I'm going to make a million by selling all the schools. I know a lot about them, and I could find some teachers and principals who might need a school."

James P., age 8

"It's good to do things for other people. It makes you feel good about yourself. So the best kind of work might be something that makes them feel good, like selling them diamond rings."

Sheila, age 8

What Is the Easiest Job in the World?

"By far, the easiest job in the world is being Prince Charles and Lady Diane. . . . They just have babies and ride their horses all day. They probably quit about three o'clock so they can stuff themselves and their brats with cupcakes and stuffy English tea. . . . It's a tough life, but somebody's got to play king and queen!"

Sylvia, age 9

"The vice-president is the easiest. . . . Especially with Dan Quayle, since he is only qualified for things like bird-watching and eating foreigners' food."

Broderick, age 10

"Easiest job? I'd say it's being a priest. You basically have to be a holy roller, and that's about it. You don't get paid for extra time you put in, but you don't have to share your money with a wife, either."

Timothy D., age 8

"A waitress is easy, because the people give you money free if they like the food, and they give you even more money if you're pretty."

Marie, age 7

"If you're a food tester, you get to try all the latest kinds of candy and cookies and see what you think. . . . I'd love it,

but I'd probably end up weighing fifty million pounds, because I wouldn't want to quit when the day was over."
Paul, age 10

"When you own an apartment house, all you have to do is bug people who live there for the rent. . . . And if they don't pay up, it's curtains for them!"
Reggie, age 9

"Being a kid is the easiest job in the world. . . . When you're a kid, all you got to work at is being good at video games!"
Mona, age 9

What Is the Hardest Job in the World?

"My mother has the hardest job. . . . She has six kids!"
Willie, age 8

"The hardest job is being a parent to me. I like to cause trouble and get dirty, but on the other hand, I mean well!"
Jake, age 8

"Being a pilot is not easy, because it takes a lot of know-how to fit one of the big planes right into the airport terminal."
Will, age 7

" A doctor is the hardest, because they have to memorize all the parts of the body and then go find them when they do the operation."

Claude, age 10

" I wouldn't want to be a college professor because you're always teaching a class that's more interested in social life than learning. . . . In my opinion, it's disgusting!"

Laura T., age 9

" It's hard to be a model even though most people think it's easy. My friend's older sister is one, so I know about it. You have to stand up straight and smile even though you might have gas or have to go to the bathroom. . . . I wouldn't like to do something where I couldn't go to the bathroom if I had to. I need some freedom."

Sandy H., age 8

" Building bridges is hard, because you might have to bring a lot of water in to put under it."

Kenny G., age 6

" Being a referee in hockey is tough. You have to skate real good, and then when you're done skating, you have to break up fights and punch out the ones who have blood on their fists. Then the rough ones go to the penalties box, and they yell at you . . . things like: 'Hey, four eyes, I'm inno-

cent! You're a lousy referee, and you skate like an old hag!'
That makes it a tough job."

Allan, age 10

Work Quiz I:
What Does a Stockbroker Do?

"They are the ones that break down the big blocks of wood
and cement so that the other guys can make the big buildings out of them. . . . They work with their hands and with
tools."

Jonathan, age 7

"They're the people they hire to clean up the mess after an
earthquake."

Sheila, age 8

"Stockbrokers? It doesn't sound like a job. . . . It sounds
more like an old cowboy show on television. Like where
they ride in with horses, and there's a whole gang of them."

Paul, age 9

"A stockbroker is a lady who makes stockings. . . . All kind
of stockings—white, blue, and even coffee-colored stockings. They make them so they don't have runs in them."

Lana, age 7

"It might be the people who train horses for the Kentucky Derby."

Philip, age 10

"It might be part of some foreign sport that we don't know about here. Like we have linebackers in football, in some other country they might have stockbrokers for a sport. [*What might a stockbroker do?*] Maybe tackle people like a linebacker does."

Reggie, age 9

"Stockbrokers live on Wall Street in a rich district with fancy houses and dogs that are all dressed up in fur coats."

Allan, age 10

"I think it has something to do with money, but other than that, I don't know if it's a legal thing or something that's a crime."

Howard, age 8

"A stock person takes money that you give them, and they try to use it to make more money for you. . . . Like if you give them five hundred dollars, they try to get you fifty thousand dollars for it."

Jamie, age 10

Concerning People Who Are Overpaid

"The hotels are all paid too much. It costs you hundreds of
dollars to stay there, and then you have to leave right after
you wake up!"

Cathy L., age 10

"My brother gets too much. . . . He's only ten, and he gets
a ten-dollar allowance!"

Will, age 7

"Baseball players got real fat wallets. . . . But a lot of them
just sit on the bench, or they just take their positions and
sit down on the field and say, 'That's nice. The other team
just scored another run. What a nice day it is because I'm
making twelve thousand dollars today!' "

Dick T., another disgrun-
tled Red Sox fan, age 8

"Doctors don't do much, because a lot of people who say
they are sick are just faking. . . . But the doctors get
paid from the insurance company for doing nothing.
. . . I know because my uncle is a doctor, and he admit-
ted it to me."

Rachel, age 9

"The art teacher makes too much. . . . All she does is make clay statues, and then she keeps looking at her watch while we sweat it out over what to do for our projects."

Valerie, age 9

"Landlords make billions. But God will get them because they're all evil!"

Regina, age 9

"It costs too much to take a train to New York. You have to save up a lot to go. . . . With all that the train company charges, you would think they would clean up that station there!"

Mona, age 9

"The mayor gets more than he should. . . . They should pay him twenty dollars for every drug pusher he puts in jail, and that's it. . . . Let him earn his money!"

Reggie, age 9

About People Who Are Underpaid

"The firemen should make a million bucks, and they shouldn't have to pay no taxes. [*Why do you feel that way?*] Because when I grow up, I'm going to be one of them!"

Eddie, age 6

"Teachers deserve more, because they're smart and they try to make us smart, and besides, education is important since a few of us might end up being winners."

Tanya, age 8

"What do astronauts make for their salaries? . . . I hope they are paid well. . . . They have to spend a lot of time upside down, and they have to eat that squishy stuff that is not exactly great food."

Marge T., age 10

"Teenagers don't get enough money when they work at places like McDonald's. The owners think they can get away with it because the teenagers are young. That's not fair. There should be a law against it . . . even if a lot of teenagers are pretty weird."

Regina, age 9

"Pilots should make more. When they go up on a big flight to California or to Japan, they never know if they're going to make it back, because some of the airplanes are so old, and there's always a crash or two every year. . . . If I was them, I wouldn't take the pay in cash, since I wouldn't want to carry it on the plane. Have them put it somewhere safe."

Paul, age 9

"Pet store owners are underpaid because nobody wants to buy their pets anymore. . . . It's real sad, and somebody should do something about it. . . . I bet the pets would pay for their own freedom if they could."

Frieda, age 8

Concerning Mom's and Dad's Jobs

" I don't know what they do, but I wish they could do something that would make me rich. . . . That will be the day!"

Carla, age 6

" My mother's job is top secret. . . . I can't tell unless I'm paid to talk!"

Charlotte, age 6

" My father is a businessman. [*What does he do?*] He has a big office, and he sits there and makes sure it looks neat, but pretty much nobody comes in beside his secretary, and I think she might be there for an hour at a time."

Kyle R., age 6

" I forgot what you call what my mother does, but I know for sure it's a filthy job."

Jamie, age 10

" I don't tell them what jobs they should have as long as they make enough to buy me plenty of hamburgers!"

Garrett, age 5

"My dad is a real estate agent. He tries to sell people houses that are empty and not fixed up yet. . . . The people like those better, because they don't want somebody's used chairs and couches. [*How much do the houses cost?*] My dad says they have to cost a lot for him to get money out of it, so I think maybe the houses might cost about five hundred dollars. . . . Maybe six hundred with the couches in it already."

George, age 8

"My mother is just a housewife. . . . You have a problem with that?"

Angelica, age 7

"My father works for a newspaper. I'm very proud of him, but I don't like to read it, because I don't like to get my hands dirty. Why do they make them like that?"

Karen J., age 8

"Both of my parents work real hard. My father is a pharmacist, and my mom is a teacher. . . . But I'm the next generation, so I don't plan on working so hard."

Allan, age 10

"My mom's a nurse. She watches over a lot of sick people, but she also sticks them with needles when she has to. . . . That's why I try to be nice to her when she gets home."

Anita, age 9

Why Don't Children Work?

"If kids worked, who would go to all the schools every day?"

Lana, age 7

"If children worked, would we have to give the money we earned to the adults? That's what I would want to know!"

Howard, age 8

"Most children are too small to work. But I know a kid who is ten years old, and he's almost got his own company. [*He must be really smart.*] Not really. He just knows a lot of adults."

Erica, age 7

"Kids don't work because we don't know how. We don't have to learn that until at least third grade."

Lizzie, age 6

"Kids are too smart to work. Let the parents do it! That's my attitude!"

Riley, age 9

"If children worked, they would never learn any math or science or how to spell . . . because most of the jobs don't have anything to do with that."

Chrissy, age 7

What Kind of Job Would You Like to Have When You Grow Up?

"I'm going to drive the school bus. I'll be real popular. I'll pick the kids up in the morning, and then I'll drive them right past the school—all the way to Dunkin' Donuts for some of those good jelly ones. . . . Don't worry, I'll get them to the school just in time for lunch!"

Joe, age 10

"I'm already an author. I wrote a book called *Sleeping Betty.* It's like *Sleeping Beauty,* but I changed her name so that it would be original."

Mona, age 9

"I might like to be a teacher. . . . The only problem is you are stuck with thirty kids all day, but I would just send them to my father if they were behavior problems. He'd know what to do with them, because when he yells it always works on me and my sister."

Lana, age 7

"I want to be a doctor, since I hear they make at least twenty-two dollars a week, and none of them ever visits your house anymore either."

Susan, age 8

"Maybe a doctor for kids. I sure don't want to be a dentist. I couldn't take it spending all day in a person's mouth—especially if they were old and didn't really have any teeth!"

Jeremy, age 8

"I hope to be a television reporter. . . . They get to dress up and wear makeup just like actors. They don't even have to remember their lines because they can read them, and all they got to do is keep smiling even if they're standing over a dead person. . . . Seems like a good living to me!"

Kirsten, age 10

"I don't want no job where you're just playing and messing around all the time. I want a serious job! [*For example?*] Like maybe a brain surgeon or else one of those people who organizes all the big boxing matches."

Rico, age 9

"Police is good, but I don't want to get shot at, so maybe I'll make movies about it and get to wear a uniform anyway. I'm not looking for glory, just a piece of the action."

Reggie, age 9

"I'm gonna be a singer, because I got the God-given talent for it. . . . Ask anybody in my neighborhood!"

Emil, age 7

How Many Hours a Day Will You Work, and How Much Money Will You Make?

"I'll work for about half an hour every day. I might get tired after that. . . . I think it's good to make about a million dollars a year."

Tawny, age 8

"Twenty-three hours every day of the week. Everybody needs a little rest!"

Jeremy, age 8

"I plan on working about a hundred and twenty-five hours a day, because you can get a lot of money for that. . . . You might even get ten dollars, so you could get as much as fifty by Christmastime!"

Larry, age 7

"You should work for about three hours and eat lunch for about four. . . . If your work is good, you can get your own diamond expense account!"

Carla, age 6

"A person should work thirty hours a day. [*But aren't there only twenty-four in a day?*] Well, there's going to have to be a lot of changes if I have my way. . . . For that kind of hard work, I expect to make a lot. [*How much a year?*] Plenty. At least two hundred dollars a year. I might have a few Kelvin Juniors by then, and you never know when you might need a new sports car."

Kelvin, age 8

"I don't know how much I'll have to work, but I hope to make a thousand dollars. . . . I actually have a lot of money already. More than even my mother has. I have a gigantic bank account. I have nine thousand dollars I can tell you about, but a lot more is stashed away, and I'm not ever going to tell you where. . . . Even if you give me an extra magic marker and it's orange, my favorite color."

Marie, age 7

"I won't have to work, because I'll be rich. I'll be able to spend about ten million dollars every month! But if I have a family, that costs money, and I might need a two-family house and a swimming pool. . . . So it would be okay to sell some lemonade in the front yard to make some more money."

Jay B., age 7

"I'll work about five hours and make my wife work eight. . . . I'm for ladies' rights! . . . We should make about fifty grand that way. To be fair, we'll split it even!"

Paul, age 9

Work Quiz II:
What Is a Politician?

"Politicians heal people and use strange medicines on them that always seem to work . . . but nobody knows how."

Bart, age 8

"They hand Kleenex to people when they are sad and listen to their problems."

Samantha G., age 8

"It sounds like something that is dirty. . . . I don't want to know about it."

Lizzie, age 6

"It might be a man who does women's hair and makes it look good."

Carla, age 6

"Politicians are okay, but you don't find them in most people's families."

Carl, age 10

"President Bush is one. They run the government, and on election day, they try to get people to go out in the rain and vote for them. They make the laws and then change them when they don't like them. . . . I think the senators are politicians, too, but they don't get much of a vote since they're not Republicans."

Sheila, age 8

"Politicians are very nice folks who come from far away and try to learn our way of talking."

Marie, age 7

The Can't-Miss Way
to Get a Raise at Work

"Don't ever come out and say that you want more money, because you will never get it then. You have to play it cool. Act like you might even quit and find another job. The place where you work might get scared, and they might even say to you: 'Yo, Carolyn. You're doing a fine job. How about a raise? Won't you stay a little longer here with us?' "

Carolyn, age 9

"Get one of those big signs and keep walkin' outside the building until they give you a raise. . . . The sign should say: BOYCOTT THIS PLACE. IT STINKS. AND I SHOULD KNOW, BECAUSE I WORKED HERE FOR TEN YEARS! . . . Even if you only been there for two or three years, it's good to exaggerate, since it will catch the people's attention."

Reggie, age 9

" If you want more salary, you could try to work on Saturdays and Sundays. . . . But I would have to tell them I have to be home early on Saturday, because I don't want to miss my favorite TV show, *227,* and I would like to see *The Golden Girls,* too."

Cynthia K., age 7

" Gargle with Listerine and see if that makes a difference."

Pete R., age 8

"Tell your boss that you think you're worth a million, and then see what he says."

Shelly, age 8

"Work real hard, and sooner or later they are bound to pay you more, because you'll be the only one in the place working hard."

Anita, age 9

"Try to impress the company with your pleasant personality, and if that doesn't work, tell them that your father owns another company that can buy them out."

Cam, age 10

" If you want to get a raise at work, just get in the elevator and push the button. . . . You'll go right to the top!"

Allan, age 10

What Would You Do if You Didn't Like Your Boss?

"Invite the big ninny over for dinner, and then cook his food raw!"

Jane, age 9

"Start a scandal about the boss and some other guy at work!"

Stephanie G., age 9

"Wait till the boss goes on vacation, and then ask for a raise from the person under him."

Trevor, age 8

"I might try to talk with him and see what the trouble is. [*What if the boss was a woman?*] I'd never talk to her. I'd be too embarrassed. . . . Also, she might yell at me like my mother does and say I should work harder at my homework if I want an allowance."

Howard, age 8

"The only way to get even with the boss is to throw a spitball at him when he's not looking. . . . A paper airplane might work if you write on it something scary like You're going to jail for cheating the customers, because I'm telling!"

Bart, age 8

"I would move to a different house and let my mother argue with him, since I'm probably going to be working for my dad."

Michael K., age 10

"I'll tell you one thing, I'd forget about the boss on his birthday and make sure everybody else did, too. . . . Let him put a candle in one of them tiny Hostess cakes instead of a nice birthday cake. . . . He'll be sorry when there's nobody singing 'Happy Birthday' to him!"

Kirsten, age 10

How Do Most People Feel About Their Work?

"You should ask somebody else. . . . I'm unemployed right now. Ask somebody with a job!"

Will, age 7

"My idea about work is that most adults are lazy and don't like to work, but they have to so they can pay for their condos and microwaves!"

Morton, age 7

"I don't like to talk about work and neither does my mother. . . . Let's talk about boys and men and romance."

Lana, age 7

". . . . ."

"A few grown-ups might like their work, but you'll never find a kid who likes his homework . . . I guarantee it!"

Susan, age 8

"I'll tell you the truth. . . . My father's only in it [*work*] for the money!"

Tawny, age 8

"It's all up to what you do. If you're a banker or an executive, you might like your work, because you make a lot of money, and you get to fly around on those corporate jets. . . . But if you're a maid or a miner or a farmer, you don't get to go anywhere. So it's pretty likely that you'll just decide that work is not a lot of fun, and you'll start planning to quit as soon as you can . . . like the next week."

Jennifer T., age 9

"My parents like what they're doing because they love to hear the sound of the cash register ticking. . . . I don't mind either, because I get stuff that means a lot to me, like my Fine Young Cannibals album."

Paul, age 9

"Some people like to work, but there's not much choice they have. . . . You can be sure that if they had a choice, they'd be standing in line for tickets to Hawaii, and they'd be all geared up to do those wild hip dances they do there."

Tara, age 8

On Why People Say "Thank God It's Friday!"

"Friday might be some kind of special religious holiday for some people . . . probably the kind that's like a festival."
Theresa B., age 8

"Maybe Fridays are just lucky for the people who say that. . . . Of course, if it was Friday the 13th, then it would be a different story!"
Corinne, age 8

"The adults say that because they like to watch *Dallas* and see all the sex that's going on there!"
Kelvin, age 8

"Kids might say that because school is out for the week, and they can finally get some fresh air."
Michael J., age 7

"People are happy at the end of the week because *Captain N. The Game Master* cartoons are on every Saturday!"
Cynthia T., age 7

"Whoever says it must be a big fish-eater. [*Fish-eater?*] Yeah, they can get all-you-eat-fish at the Ground Round every

Friday. . . . It's all right, but I like the buffalo wings on Wednesdays a lot better."

Carl P., age 8

"The workers are glad as heck the week is over, and so they can go home and be with their wives and their children. They have a good time up till Sunday, when about two o'clock they start to cry and get real depressed because the next day is Monday, and they'll be suffering all over again."

Allan, a budding sociologist,
age 10

Work Quiz III:
What Does an Architect Do?

"Architects? They're the ones you see in movies like *Indiana Jones*. . . . They search for dead bodies, bones, and sometimes stray dogs."

Mona, age 9

"Maybe they help doctors with the operations, or maybe they are the guys who drive the ambulance when you dial 911."

Stacy, age 8

"They work with animals and clean them good. A lot of people wouldn't want to do it because of the smell."

Gerard, age 7

"Mostly they just draw pictures and color them in to look like buildings."

Susan, age 8

"It might be one of those jobs of the future. Like if they ever start a new country on the moon, they'll need all kinds of special people. . . . This might be one of them. Maybe an architect is supposed to fill in the craters, or else be on the lookout for moonies!"

Howard, age 8

A Short List of Things That Are Unquestionably More Terrible Than Work

"Being married to Sean Penn!"

Mona, age 9

"Being in a jungle where the lions and tigers haven't had a good steak in months!"

Reggie, age 9

"Playing for the Cowboys would be worse than working, because they only won one game last year since they fired that bald guy."

Jeremy, age 8

"Probably it would be worse to live in another country, like South America. You might not be able to get a job, and you'd have to stand in line for hours just to buy a bagel!"

Howard, age 8

"Getting a shot at the doctor's is worse."

Lana, age 7

"I would rather work at a regular job than smuggle something illegal. . . . If you do something illegal, you don't get no life insurance either."

Rico, age 9

"Being in the same house as my sister is more terrible. She's a maniac, and she's always giving me a hassle for being sloppy. . . . At least at work, you get paid for your troubles!"

Paul, age 9

The Great Debate: Should Women Work at the Same Jobs as Men Do?

"Sure . . . Let them suffer, too!"

Allan, age 10

"No, women shouldn't work so much, because they need to be pregnant most of the time, and that makes it hard for them to bend down."

Bart, age 8

"I would put them on the construction jobs right off and see how they do."

Joe, age 10

"No, there's only some jobs that women can do. . . . Like being the president and running the Supreme Court!"

Kirsten, age 10

"I think what's fair is fair. That means everybody is equal, and nobody should have to pick up after anybody . . . especially if the messy ones are men!"

Anita, age 9

"Girls should do all the jobs, but not the ones that have violence in them. . . . That's for men like me!"

Joe, age 8

"The best jobs for the ladies are the jobs that don't mess up their hair and their faces."

Will, age 7

"If the women want to, it's okay with me. But I wouldn't force them, because they might get real angry and not cook anything."

Larry, age 7

"Women are supposed to take care of the kids, but they work a lot, too. When are they supposed to get a rest? Still, we got a right to be the same as men—even if we're double tough as they are and don't even complain about it by saying: 'My foot hurts, darling. Will you rub it for me, please?'"

Shelly, age 8

"Women can do what the men do. I would say to a man, right to his face: 'Move over, bud, I'm taking your job!'"

Randi, age 8

Work Quiz IV:
What Does a Psychiatrist Do?

"If you have a lot of money, they call you and ask if you can help them out with a donation. . . . They tell you it's for a good cause."

Gloria J., age 9

"They take care of your feet and tell you to use Dr. Scholl's foot spray."

Anita, age 9

"Maybe they take care of pets and make sure they aren't sick, or they see if their hands and feet are okay."

Bart, age 8

"They might sell you insurance if you're an adult, and if you're a kid, they say, 'Now, run along and go get your parents for me.'"

Rhonda, age 8

"If you're wacko, they try to talk you into being normal!"

Joe, age 10

"The guy on *Cheers* is one. . . . He listens to people's problems, like they do at the bar. He's always clowning with Sam about girl problems, and then they have a good joke about sex."

Allan, age 10

"Psychs are persons who try to predict the future by what month you are born. Some of them just fake it, and people still believe them."

Reggie, age 9

How Is Work Different in
Other Countries?

"In Asia, they work more hours and get less pay. They might get rice instead of dollars. . . . I would rather have dollars, because it gives you more choice, and also rice sticks together a lot."

Brooke, age 10

"I don't know how it would be different except some may have farms and animals . . . and they may not rush around all the time and complain they are stressed out and take headache medicine for it."

Charles, age 10

"Maybe they got to pay money to their president, and they don't get days like July 4th off."

Jonathan, age 7

"They probably trade stuff instead of the way we do it here. Like if you're a fix-it guy, you might fix something at another guy's house. But he doesn't write you a check. Instead, he gives you something for it. Like some food or maybe an animal, such as a pig to make pork chops out of it. The harder the fix-it job, the bigger the pig."

Shelton, age 8

"They got the same jobs as we do in Italy, but they sleep more during the day than we do."

Albert, age 9

"They got more hockey jobs in Canada."

Howard, age 8

"They could work with their families in some countries. They might be old-fashioned. They all work together, even the kids, and then they're all tired at the end of the day, and so they say to each other: 'Sayonara, bedtime'!"

Riley, age 9

On the Serenity of Retirement

"I'm going to retire when I'm sixteen. That's when I'm giving up this boring paper route."

Mark C., age 9

"Most grandparents save their money and then go to Las Vegas when they retire, because they like to live it up before it's too late."

Melissa, age 8

"Some people miss their jobs, but the ones who get ESPN are happy like anything, because they can just sit home and watch sports all day!"

Reggie, age 9

"I'm going to work when I'm a hundred. I love money too much to quit when I'm still wild and fun."

Eddie, age 6

"I think it's a good idea to have a retired persons thing, so you don't have to work forever. By the time you're forty, many people want to just throw up at their jobs."

Jeremy, age 8

"Most of the older people go to Florida, and they never come back except to visit. To them, New England is like Alaska, and they don't want any more of those blizzards. . . . Also, they like the beaches even though their shapes aren't so good any more."

Joe, age 10

"I plan to get a lot of rest and maybe just wash my car every day. If I want to earn some extra money, I might sell old furniture in the yard or try out the horse races. I could get lucky and pick an old horse who needs the money, too."

Howard, age 8

Those New Jobs That Will Be Created
by the Time They Grow Up—Sometime in
the Next Century

"I'll have my own robot. I'll call him Charles. And he'll get things for me out of the refrigerator, and then he'll say: 'Is there anything else, sir?' "

Paul, age 9

"You know how the actors and sports people have their own agents? Well, every single person will have an agent by then. So, if you work at a store like Woolworth's, you'll still have an agent to say you should get more money, or he might complain if you slip on a greasy floor."

Allan, age 10

"There will be more nature artists, people who draw the nature scenes. . . . The way it's going now with the land, nature is only going to be a drawing or just somebody's memories."

Albert, age 9

"There will be schedule people to figure out when it's your turn to go to heaven."

Mona, age 9

223

"There might be more people to write down what kids say. By then, they will see that what kids have to say is real important."

Sheila, age 8

"There will be married priests in the future, and that means a lot of Mrs. Priests, who will make sure that the priests dress with a little more color but still do the same good masses."

Mary Beth, age 8

"They will have people-counters to count all the people. And they'll have to have more numbers to figure it all out. . . . They might use letters to cover some of the ones who live way out in the ocean."

Bobby, age 8

"They'll have to hire special trash people to pick up stuff around the universe—especially Milky Way bars!"

Riley, age 9

"We won't need doctors anymore because we'll be so healthy. Instead, we'll get the medicine we need from machines like candy machines or soda machines. . . . Like you put in fifty cents, and you get an aspirin or diet aspirin."

Cam, age 10

. . . .

"The police won't have to carry regular guns anymore. They just point a special laser at you, and in a second, you stop stealing and you start helping old people cross the street, you visit people who are sick and you give money to the homeless."

Valerie, age 9

"There'll be people who have the job of teaching other people to do the right thing . . . and those people will teach other people, too, and pretty soon, it will all spread around the world."

Reggie, age 9

VI

"Growing Up Isn't Hard to Do if You Start Out as a Kid!" (and Other Philosophical Thoughts About Growing Up)

"I don't know if growing up is hard or not, because I have not seen many examples of it yet."
Taylor, age 7

All of the preceding chapters have concerned specific aspects of the adult world. Each selection is a window into how children see adults, and their parents in particular. Despite our best efforts to categorize children's comments and ideas, some of their original offerings defy simple description. The observations that follow concern the growing-up process in general, and thus provide an even richer appreciation of the child's philosophical vantage point.

If an adult is "a child blown up by age," as Simone de Beauvoir contended, then adults are parading in full view of their youngsters, like Mickey Mouse and Garfield do in the Macy's Thanksgiving Day Parade. Grown-ups reveal adult habits and say adult things for their children to copy; the parent's version of adulthood is taken in and considered carefully by the child. Children want to know what the process of growing up is like, so they study adults with a certain amazement. Bemused by adult eccentricities, the youngsters are captivated by how all this change happens to a person.

Children are eager to entertain questions about what adulthood is like and how it feels to be a grown-up. They will speculate about what it takes to grow up and whether most adults are really happy. The children even comment on the many things that they can teach adults, and whether or not growing up is truly hard to do.

Ultimately, the kids can't resist telling a story or two about grown-ups—colorful vignettes complete with lifelike characters who are suspiciously parent-like in demeanor. Oh, the stories about their parents that kids can tell, and how wonderfully willing they are to tell them! Let's see what the kids have to say about growing up.

When Does a Child Officially Become an Adult?

"You have to be tall, and you have to take showers by yourself."

Carey H., age 5

"It's when you have your own bottle of hair spray."

Mindy, age 7

"You can become an adult when you graduate from a place like Harvard or Boston University and you get your diploma and you throw it like a paper airplane glider."

Sid, age 8

"At twenty, you become instantly cool, and you might even have a house to show for it."

Valerie, age 9

". . . . ."

"If the guy at the bank is nice to you, that probably means you have moved up to being an adult."

Roland, age 10

"You aren't really grown-up unless you have your own hair dryer!"

Emma, age 7

"You are not a child if either you get married or you get your driver's license—whichever one comes first."

Marie, age 7

"You got to be able to go to the bathroom on your own."

Lizzie, age 6

"I'm grown-up right now. . . . I'm just short for a grown-up!"

Pierce, age 7

"You are pretty grown-up when you know that birds and bees are not just regular creatures."

Rhonda, age 8

"When you're sixteen, you can drive your mom and dad around and show them what's it's like to have to sit in the backseat for a change!"

Sheila, age 8

"There's no one time you are already an adult, but I would say it happens around the time you go to your senior prom."

Shelly, age 8

"It might be about thirty. You got to quit exploring then and figure out how to get out of the mess your life could be in."

Martin J., age 10

"When you're ten, that's pretty much it. You can't play with toys no more."

Jason, age 5

"Everybody grows up at a different time. There's no one way. Some kids are grown-up when they're thirteen. . . . I know some kids that are rich brats who just play up to rich Mommy and Daddy, and they get anything they want. Those kids will never make it on their own. . . . Even if I was rich, I wouldn't hang around at home after high school is over. I plan on being independent. I'm just that kind of guy."

Reggie, age 9

"I will be an adult when they start calling me Mr. Ben instead of just plain Ben."

Mr. Ben, age 6

What Do You Think It Feels Like
to Be a Grown-up?

"Ask our teacher, Mr. Reynolds. . . . He might be one."
Evan, age 8

"It might be okay, but I wouldn't give up being a kid to try it out!"
Marie, age 7

"You might feel big for a while, but then you would run into your mother and that would all change!"
Harold, age 7

"Being a grown-up would feel like a million bucks! You're real tall and you can see the world better. You don't got to climb on anybody else."
Brian, age 6

"It would feel great to be a grown-up on payday!"
Riley, age 9

"It might be neat to be a grown-up for a day, but I wouldn't want to do it forever."
Anita, age 9

"You probably feel a lot like children do, but you can't just show how you feel all the time. . . . How would it look if an adult had a temper tantrum and they started yellin': 'I want my way! I want my way!' "

Howard, age 8

"You must feel like you have a big headache all the time if your job is stressful and if your kids are more than you count on one of your hands."

Kirsten, age 10

"You should ask my mother. . . . She's being a grown-up for plenty of years."

Mindy, age 7

"I think a lot of them feel like they wish they were young again so they can have a lot of good times. But most kids like me can't wait until we are grown-up. . . . Maybe the people in-between got it best."

Quinn, age 8

Do You Think That Most Grown-ups Are Happy?

"You can't really say for sure. There's too many of them walking around on the earth to keep track of them all."

Candace W., age 7

"Happy? They are when you lie to them and tell them they look good, even when they're fifty years old."

Rhonda, age 8

"My mother and father are happy, because they have the cutest kids in the world. . . . It's not bragging when you can back it up."

Sheila, age 8

"I think grown-ups are happy if they go to those happy hours after they quit working."

Kally, age 9

"They should be happy. They own all the bank accounts!"

Eddie, age 6

"They're happy if they can take a pile of vacations and also if they can go take a sauna every day."

Howard, age 8

"If you go by TV, then they are happy. But I think some aren't. Why else would they be mean to people they don't know, or else be mean to the kids they do know?"

Bill, age 9

"I wouldn't be too keen on coming home at eight o'clock every night, either. . . . So I think that makes it hard to be happy, but they can still be happy if they follow sports and they know how to sing."

Carlos, age 10

"I think my mother's happy, but my father's kind of moody. So I would say they're half happy. . . . I tell my father to chill out, but he doesn't always listen to me."

Marti, age 10

"They could be happy if they like to draw and color a lot. That's what I do in my spare time."

Cindy, age 6

If You Saw a Person That You Didn't Know Walking Down the Street, How Could You Tell if That Person Was Totally Grown Up?

"If they're bald, there's a pretty good chance that they might be grown-up."

Martin J., age 10

"If they are Italian, they probably are grown up. Most Italian people I know like my grandma and grandpa, the ones that come from my mom, are real old."

Hilary, age 8

"Take a look and find out if they got kids hanging on their backs."

Harold, age 7

"Check and see if they have a grown-up shoe size."

Carey H., age 5

"They are grown up if their heads are big. . . . A grown-up is just a kid with a bigger head, and maybe he wears glasses, too."

Emma, age 7

"Ask them if they hate school."

Joey T., age 9

"You could tell by the clothes they are wearing. Some might have a suit or a dress on. . . . But probably not if they do something like play hockey."

Albert, age 9

"Grown up is not something you can tell on the outside. . . . You have to know how much money they make and how much they carry on the inside of their pockets."

Ron B., age 10

"...

"They definitely won't be chewing gum no more, and they might not eat candy, either. . . . That's why I'm staying put!"
Regina, age 8

"You're grown up if you like buying toys for the kids; you're not grown up if they like getting the toys better."
Sheri, age 9

"If the person is walking in a hurry, it's probably a person who's all grown up. . . . A child would not be in such a big hurry to get home, because they know they're going to have to do their homework when they do."
Susan, age 8

"If they can still run fast, they are probably still teenagers. Ask the people to have a race, and time them with a watch. Then you can know for sure."
Ben, future Olympic timer, age 6

If There Was One Thing You Could Change About Grown-ups, What Would It Be?

"I'd make them smaller so they would be about the same size as children."
Elizabeth, age 4

". . . . ."

"I would make it so they didn't have to work, so we could take more trips to places like Plimoth Plantation."
Cindy, age 6

"When they get paid, they should admit it and say, 'Come on, let's all go to Wendy's!'"
Susan, age 8

"I'd like to change the time they wake me up in the morning . . . Seven-thirty . . . A kid can't get any sleep."
Eddie, age

"My mother needs a new hairdo. . . . Other than that, I can't think of anything."
Meryl, age 9

"Grown-ups should joke more. Kids know how to have a good time, but grown-ups need some lessons. . . . Maybe they should go to a comedy club."
Carol L., age 8

"I think all grown-ups should have to answer to a bigger power . . . my grandparents!"
Earl B., age 10

···

"No adult, especially my mother, should use a vacuum cleaner when her nice children are trying to watch television!"

Evan, age 8

"I would dress all of them different and make them wear the stuff that teenagers wear, like gold chains. . . . That will make them be less serious."

Sheree, age 10

"I wish that certain blonde-haired grown-ups would stop bugging me to do my homework. . . . Still, I think it's a good thing that kids have mothers."

Jeff T., age 9

"Adults should shower quicker or they should have an extra bathroom in case their children have the runs."

Jonathan W., age 8

"My dad should take more time to match his shirts and ties. My mom dresses real good, but she should help my dad more. She should say to him: 'Dear, you look nice, but you could look even nicer if you changed all your clothes.' "

Kirsten, age 10

Are You Looking Forward
to Being Grown Up?

"There's no fool like an old fool."
                              Cam, age 10

"I'm lookin' forward to it. I'm tired of having to go to bed before everybody else."
                              Matthew J., age 6

"I'm not in any big hurry. . . . I like the sandbox I got here, and we got a VCR. . . . If you could keep your sandbox when you grow up, then everything would be great. Because I know you can still have a VCR. . . . I might like to do it then."
                              Ben, age 6

"I can't wait. . . . I already got a big wallet, and now all I need is a little cash to put in it!"
                              Kelvin, age 8

"My father says a person should be happy wherever they are. So I'm happy being a child for now. . . . In a few years, I might be a lot happier as an adult with my own brand-new yacht."
                              Paul, age 9

....

"Yeah, I'm going to be a grown-up someday. . . . You think I'm kidding? I already know how to spell some words."

Tamara G., age 6

"It will be fun to be grown up, because I'm going to be a general and own a lot of land."

Jerry, age 5

"When I grow up, I'm going to make sure it's safe for my children. . . . I'm going to have a gun and shoot all the bad people on the block."

Arnold F., age 7

"The coolest thing about being an adult will be all the hell-raising you can do . . . especially if you're in one of those frats!"

Riley, age 9

"I'm excited about turning ten next year. . . . I can't think any farther ahead about being an adult, because I don't want to miss the fun of being a kid. . . . Ten is supposed to be a good age because you get more freedom, but nobody expects much of you yet."

Irene K., age 9

The Trouble with Not Being
Grown Up Yet

"You never get to watch all the shows you want on TV when you're a child. I always miss the end of the hockey games, because it's on the same time as *Thirtysomething.*"
Gerald, age 8

"When you're too little, you can't reach the top shelf in the kitchen without getting the big stool."
Cindy, age 6

"You can't own your own Fortune 500 company!"
Cam, age 10

"You can't pick your own beliefs; you got to go along with your parents. . . . At least until you get your license, and then everything changes and you can believe what you want."
Andi, age 8

"Nothing is bad about being a child so far. I hope it stays like that, because I don't want to put up with any mega-changes."
Tanya, age 8

"The worst thing about being a kid is having to wear hand-me-down sweaters. . . . I hate the fuzzy kind especially. . . . When I grow up, I'm going to own the whole sweater department of a store like Filene's."

Simone, age 9

"Not being grown up means you can't stay up and see the movies that make everybody giggle."

Rhonda, age 8

In What Ways Are Children and Adults Alike?

"They both walk on two legs, but that's about where the alike part ends."

Derrick, age 8

"Children and their parents might look alike if they still got the parents they started with."

Monica D., age 9

"Both can get lint in their belly buttons."

Cheri, age 6

"Both of them came down from the animals like the apes, and then they learned how to act like decent human beings . . . but the kids are still learning."

Morton J., age 9

"God loves the adults and the kids, but it takes more energy for Him to love all the adults."

Blaire, age 10

"The grown-ups and the children all got to eat and got to go to the toilet, but some of the little kids forget to flush it sometimes or else they put too much paper in, and then you got a big flood."

Marie, age 7

"They all wear Levi jeans."

Sheri, age 9

"Kids and grown-ups are not really alike. . . . Kids love it when it snows, and grown-ups grumble about what a mess it is to get their cars. They should just enjoy the snow and go sledding, instead of going to work. That's what snow days are all about. . . . Then grown-ups and kids would have more in common."

Mitchell, age 8

"It doesn't matter. . . . You could be a kid or a parent. You have to get eight hours of sleep, and you need your nap time every day."

Rita, age 7

"Everybody likes to have a good laugh and feel good. And they like to eat popcorn, too. But some kids don't like to share the popcorn, and the grown-up parent has to share, because that's her kids who are grabbing for the bowl."

Sheila, age 8

What Are Some of the Things That Children Can Teach Grown-ups?

"How to make a sand castle at the beach."

Cindy, age 6

"We can teach them how to behave in front of *their* parents. . . . My grandmother would really appreciate that!"

Roland, age 10

"Kids know more than grown-ups about wrist-wrestling and riding bikes—there's no grown-up who knows more than us."

Kelvin, age 8

"We need to teach them more about how to teach."

Olivia, age 8

" Most kids are better at baseball . . . but some grown-ups like my father think they are Roger Clemens when they're throwing the ball!"

Grant, age 8

" Children can teach their parents not to be idiots and to put their seat belts on every time!"

Martin J., age 10

" Kids always know where the best waterslides are and where to find an ice cream truck that sells bomb pops."

Sheri, age 9

" Adults should learn how to play dodgeball, and then they might have less wars."

Will, age 7

" Kids can teach their mother arithmetic . . . because the mother always spends too much at the grocery store because she loses track of how much the food is."

Howard, age 8

" Kids can do anything. You just name it. But they shouldn't be too hard on their parents if their parents are lame.

. . . .

". . . It happens to everybody when they get to be as old as forty."

Paul, age 9

"We could teach them how to be better parents by not yelling when we have our own children, even if they should break a window and ruin the grass."

Carly, age 8

"Teach them what? . . . It's too late for that with most of the grown-ups I know real well."

Rhonda, age 8

"I would like to teach my mom and dad to enjoy playing Nintendo. . . . Then we'd have more to do together."

Lonnie, age 9

Growing Up Is Hard to Do Because . . .

"It's easy to get a disease along the way."

Martin J., age 10

"Growing up is hard, because all the time I'm growing up, I got to raise my doll, too. . . . And my doll Trudi wets a lot!"

Cindy, age 6

. . . .

"Growing up isn't hard to do if you have a hit record by the time you are a teenager!"

Vance, age 8

"Being a grown-up is hard, because toys cost a lot these days."

Ben, age 6

"Once you get to six, you have a whole bunch of worries."

Lizzie, age 6

"You only have your parents to learn from, and they aren't perfect, either!"

Reggie, age 9

"You aren't born with a set of directions the way a computer is."

Carlos, age 10

"Growing up isn't hard to do if you start out as a kid, because you can learn a lot, and you probably won't forget it, at least until you're older."

Carrie B., age 8

"Growing up is hard, since you cannot always get your way every time, and so it takes a lot of brain power to figure out how to get your way."

Seth, age 10

"Once you start being grown up, there's no way to quit or stop and try it all over again."

Blaire, age 10

"Growing up is hard if you're against it for personal reasons."

Riley, age 9

"It's hard to grow up if you're alone, but if you got a husband, maybe he can do some of the grown-up things for you."

Susan, age 8

"No way I'm going to grow up until I finish college. . . . You got to have a good education first!"

Rita, age 7

"Growing up is hard to do, because you have to start paying for your clothes."

Mindy, age 7

"I don't know if growing up is hard because I have not seen many examples of it yet."

Taylor, age 7

"Growing up is hard so I might try something else . . . like working as a camp counselor and playing kids' games all the time."

George, age 8

Which Grown-up Do You *Most* Admire?

"I admire Freddy Krueger because he's in a lot of movies, and he gets to meet a lot of different people . . . at least for a little while."

Will, age 7

"President Bush—he's a good leader, and he's made the most out of being rich."

Nancy T., age 9

"I like all of the Turtles, but maybe they don't count because they are teenagers."

Harold, age 7

"My mother—'cause she buys me a lot of clothes and she knows where to get the best deals. That ain't easy, ya know!"

Susan, age 8

"I admire my grandmother. All the time when it's my birthday, she always buys me the most and sometimes I get to visit her in Ohio. . . . But I hardly get anything from my parents, because they're more on the cheap side of adults."

Valerie, age 9

"I admire Michael Jordan because I would like to sky like he does, and doing all those Wheaties commercials with me on the box would be cool, too."

Riley, age 9

"I admire the pilots who fly people all around the world. How do you figure how to get to a place? I still have trouble getting around my school since they built the addition on!"

Lou, age 7

"I admire my older brother John because he's real smart. . . . You wouldn't believe it, but he knows more than me."

Marie, age 7

"Joe Montana is tops because he's won a lot of Super Bowls, and he got successful without much of an education, I think."

Howard, age 8

"I would say that it would be Mother Teresa because she is unselfish and is close to being a saint. . . . I wouldn't mind being a saint, but I don't think I would have a good enough record by the time I grow up."

Tamara, age 10

"I admire Barbara Bush. She's a nice lady, and she's real mature, and she loves her husband a lot. I think she probably helps him a lot and gives him advice. . . . My mom is like that with my dad, too. My dad isn't a president or anything, but we love him anyway."

Kirsten, age 10

Which Grown-up Do You *Least* Admire?

"The ones that are trying to sell you junk on the J.C. Penney Television Shopping station!"

Dean, age 8

"I least admire our principal. He's mean to kids, real mean. I don't think he should take it out on us just because he looks like a pit bull!"

Albert, age 9

"The worst people in the world are uncles . . . like my uncle Robbie. He gets mad at me all the time for no reason. . . . I also don't like rock 'n' roll singers, because they act like him. One time Robbie was over, and he just switched my television to MTV without asking. That just shows what lousy taste he has."

Kally, age 9

"I hate my little cousin, Vic. He's not a grown-up, but he will be one day unless I kill him first. . . . He always cries after I hit him back, and he tries to blame me."

Rudi, age 8

"Wrestlers like Macho Man Randy are terrible people. I don't understand why my mother likes them."

Ivan, age 7

"David Letterman is weird. I'm glad he's on late so he doesn't ruin the programs that I watch."

Mona, age 9

"I don't like snobs like the hotel lady they put in jail. . . . But I didn't think they could arrest you for just being a jerk."

Arthur C., age 9

. . . .

"I hate drug pushers the most, and second place would probably go to phony people like Geraldo."

Anita, age 9

"Donald Trump needs to get his personality fixed!"

Kirsten, age 10

"Prince is getting old and so is Madonna. . . . Paula Abdul
is good because she is still young."

Renee D., age 8

"The people I least admire are all the dictators and people
who don't believe in democracy. They're not grown-ups at
all. . . . I bet they were real troublemakers when they were
kids."

Susan, age 8

What Grade Would You Give to Grown-ups for How Well They're Running the World?

"What makes you think they are the ones running the world?
. . . It's all just a matter of a few years before we take it
over!"

Reggie, age 9

....

"I'd give them all D's. . . . Well, maybe I'd be an easy teacher and give them D+'s. . . . Do you know what they should do? They should send all of the grown-ups to school, and we'll drive them there on our way to work!"

Mitchell R., age 8

"Maybe a B . . . The grown-ups put in a lot of effort, but the whole world is still sloppy!"

Wendy, age 8

"C— . . . People should be helping each other instead of yelling at each other."

Valerie, age 9

"I'd have to give them an Incomplete—they have much more work to do."

Shelly, age 8

"I might have to give the grown-ups an A because if I didn't, I might have to make my dinner on my own."

Will, age 7

"F! There's too many homeless people. Everybody should be ashamed of themselves. Nobody's even trying. . . . I think if it was school, you would have to make the whole world stay back a year!"

Kenneth R., age 10

A Few Everyday Stories About
Grown-ups in the '90s

"One time my mother was playing with my dad. My mother jumped on the bed and started acting like the Karate Kid. Then my father came on the bed and started laughing, too. Then all of a sudden my mother started yelling and doing karate kicks on my father.
    "I wonder why they do kid stuff like that?"

Kally, age 9

"There was three big grown-ups, and there was a little girl called Goldilocks. . . . But by mistake, Goldilocks ate all their dinners, and so they were really mad. They decided to punish her but cutting off most of her golden hair.
    "When the terrible day came, Goldilocks figured she better do somethin' quick. She was scared, but she didn't scream or anything. She used her head. By the time the three big grown-ups had come to get even with her and cut off her locks, she had already gone to the hairdresser and got her hair permed!"

Mona, age 9

"A mother and a father had three kids, but they were still bored. So they thought they would do something about it, and they said, 'By golly, let's have another toddler.' But then their own parents said, 'Oh no, you can't have another. You aren't even finished with the ones you have. They need more discipline.'
    "So the young mother and father made believe they were

being strict with their kids, and all the while they were busy producing another spanking new kid."

Kirsten, age 10

"We have a dog named Skippy that everybody loves. Only my father didn't want to get him, and I think Skippy knows it. Whenever my father is in the kitchen, there's no way Skippy will eat. He always looks around to see where my father is. Then Skippy will start eating when my father leaves the kitchen.

"Skippy is not dumb. He knows when there's a prejudiced adult around."

Ossie, age 8

"My mom and dad bought a blender, but it broke after a few months. My dad said, 'Oh, great, Laura, another expensive thing down the tubes.' And then my mother, that's Laura, says, 'We should have bought the better one. It wouldn't have broken!'

"That's the way it is at my house. . . . It's a regular soap opera, except I never get to see the sex. Some things are supposed to be for a kid's imagination."

Mallory, age 10

"My mom always leaves us a note on a little blackboard in the kitchen. One day she left us one that said: BE GOOD TO YOUR MOTHER. HOW ARE YOU GOING TO GET TO THE MALL WITHOUT HER!"

Regina, age 9

If There Was a Land Called 'Grownupsville,' Where Only Adults and No Children Lived, What Do You Think It Would Be Like?

"It would be the opposite of Kidsville, where the whole town would be full of swimming pools and waterslides and rides."

> Danny P., age 6

"Nobody would wear bows in their hair. It would be very bad."

> Cindy, age 6

"It wouldn't be too much of a tourist spot, that's for sure. Who would go there for fun?"

> Reggie, age 9

"All of the babysitters would be out of work."

> Rhonda, age 8

"In Grownupsville, the grown-ups could go to grocery stores like the giant store near my house. But they wouldn't have to use part of their carts to put their little babies in. So there would be more room for food and good stuff . . . for the young grown-ups like me."

> Carey H., age 5

"I would never go to Grownupsville because you never know, they might not have any peanut butter there!"

Molly, age 6

"There probably wouldn't be any Little League baseball unless some short grown-ups played the positions."

Harold, age 7

"It would be dull and boring, and people would watch Oprah Winfrey all the time."

Anita, age 9

"There would be skyscrapers and buildings with a lot of lights and a lot of business and a lot of fog . . . probably not much grass or clean air to breathe."

Susan, age 8

"All the town's people would miss the little people who used to bug them all the time."

Dick, age 7

"Christmas wouldn't be much fun, but the people wouldn't have to spend so much, either."

Will, age 7

....

"Without kids, there wouldn't be any schools, so nobody would know how to do math and speak English right."

Nellie, age 8

"There would be nobody to eat all the candy bars!"

Riley, age 9

"It would all be full of strange signs, and money would be everything. There would be no toy stores and no children's books. There would be no boy scouts or girl scouts. . . . It would all be like a different planet, and the people would be like alien weirdos. Like Alf but not as cute."

Carrie B., age 8

"There would be no Charlie Brown specials."

Mindy, age 7

"The marriages wouldn't last. . . . They would need the kids to spice it up."

Kirsten, age 10

"Grownupsville would probably have a lot of gambling and sex and bad stuff, because they wouldn't care, since there's no kids around to see. . . . It would be doomed unless they took in some kids."

Bobby, age 8

"The people would all die of empty hearts."

Joan K., age 9

"If there was no children and it was all adults, then they probably wouldn't have any station wagons any more, and the cars would be smaller."

Ryan, age 8

"It would be hard for movies like *Teenage Mutant Ninja Turtles* to be as popular as they are now."

Jerod, age 9

"It might be fun for a while, because the grown-ups would have more time for themselves and not have to worry about their kids. But pretty soon they'll start to miss the little tykes, and then the grown-ups will start bawling about how depressed they are. . . . You'll see a lot of FOR SALE signs before you know it, because people will be moving out of the town."

Cam, age 10

"In Grownupsville, if there was only grown-ups, they would have to start digging some underground tunnels so that they could sneak the kids in. . . . The kids could smuggle them some ice cream and soda, not to mention themselves."

Martin J., age 10

. . . .

"The people would be cleaner, but all the woods and dirt fields would go to waste."

Teddy, age 7

"There would be nobody to teach things to, so the grown-ups would have to find something else, like trying to teach their pet dogs how to read."

Dick, age 7

"There wouldn't be many balloons or puppet shows or pizza parties, so I don't think I would ever go there. If somebody invited me, I would have to say: 'No, thanks, I'm not coming to your town until you are less messed up. You need to let in some of those great kids and let them open a toy store on Main Street.' "

Jack, age 8

"Grownupsville? No kids? Just grown-ups? It will never happen. . . . God will never let it."

Eric B., age 10

ABOUT THE AUTHOR

DR. DAVID HELLER is best known for his books about children's views of the world, including their ideas about religion and politics. He has also written about such other compelling subjects as the development of manhood in *The Soul of a Man* (1990) and child care and parenting in *Talking to Your Child About God* (1990; 1988). His books have been featured selections of the Book-of-the-Month Club, the Literary Guild, the Doubleday Book Club and the Macmillan Behavioral Sciences Book Club.

Dr. Heller is a graduate of Harvard, where he received summa cum laude and Phi Beta Kappa honors and has also taught. He earned his doctorate in clinical psychology from the University of Michigan, where he first began to study children's views.

Currently, he resides in Boston with his wife, Elizabeth, and is hard at work interviewing children about a number of previously unexplored subjects.